About

Paying
For College

"*10 Things You Gotta Know About Paying for College* should make parents everywhere jump for joy. At a time when most guides focus on 'what's in it for them,' Brandon Rogers shows what's in it for everyone."

Mike Lowry, Former Washington State Governor and Congressman

"Brandon Rogers has used his own experience as a financial aid counselor to provide invaluable advice. Choosing a community or technical college path is a much less expensive option for students and parents, and Brandon shows everyone how to reach their higher education goals in a cost effective way."

Dr. Sharon McGavick, President, Clover Park Technical College

"This book is the financial aid equivalent of the film *Supersize Me*, exposing the intricacies and often the conflicting policies and disincentives for hard work and savings."

Wayne Meisel, President, Bonner Foundation

"Finally, a college guide that doesn't portray the financial aid administrator as the enemy. Students will benefit tremendously from this fresh perspective on paying for college."

Doug Severs, Financial Aid Director, Idaho State University

"Brandon Rogers pulls off something that back in college I would have thought impossible: his advice on financial aid is entertaining, while at the same time he gives students a clear route for getting the best possible aid package. You'll never look at the FAFSA the same way again."

Richard Melo, Author, *Jokerman 8*

"Having had to pay my own way through college, I could really relate to the importance of this book. It shows you the money and how to get it. What a relief this book can be on your bank account! Brandon knows his stuff!"

Patrick Combs, Author, *Major in Success: Make College Easier,*
Fire Up Your Dreams and Get a Very Cool Job*

"Congratulations, you've just discovered your proverbial pot o' gold. Brandon Rogers has developed a resource worthy of every household."

Ivey Harrison, Admissions Counselor, Presbyterian College

10 THINGS YOU GOTTA KNOW

About

Paying For College

Brandon Rogers

SPARK
COLLEGE

AN IMPRINT OF SPARK PUBLISHING

WWW.SPARKCOLLEGE.COM

Spark Publishing
A Division of Barnes & Noble Publishing
120 Fifth Avenue
New York, NY 10011
www.sparknotes.com

ISBN 1-4114-0351-7

Please submit changes or report errors to **www.sparknotes.com/errors**

Printed and bound in Canada.

Library of Congress Cataloging-in-Publication Data available upon request.

CONTENTS

Why 10 Things?

<hr>

It seems like everyone's writing books that claim to give you the basics, nice and simple—but what you get are pages overstuffed with lots of information you just don't need.

With *10 Things You Gotta Know*, we give you *exactly* what you need—no more, no less. We know you want your knowledge *now*, without wasting time on information that's not important. Learning 10 quick basics is the way to go.

Each 10 *Things* book contains:

- Lots of clear headings for skimming
- Sound bites of text that are easy to digest
- Sidebars that enhance your understanding
- Tons of Top 10 Lists for vital facts at a glance

Sure—maybe you could argue that there are 8 vital things, or 11. This isn't rocket science. But 10 is such a nice, even number—and who doesn't love a great Top 10?

In this book, we focus on the 10 things you absolutely, positively gotta know about paying for college:

1. **The Process**

   This chapter explains the terms, forms, and procedures you're going to encounter on your financial aid journey. It explains what you're qualified for—and how to get it.

2. **The Long plan**

   If you're lucky enough to have lots of time before heading off to college, then you'll benefit from the long-term strategies described in this chapter. You'll learn how to work the system well in advance to optimize your financial aid and minimize your family's contribution.

3. **The Short Plan**

   Even if college is right around the corner, there are plenty of things you can do to maximize your financial aid. In this chapter you'll learn the tricks and strategies that will help you get more and pay less.

4. **The Free Money**

   Here you'll find a veritable gold mine of resources and tips to help you find—and win—the free money that's out there to help you pay for college. Knowing where to look is half the battle.

5. **The Loans**

   Borrowing money to pay for college is par for the course these days, and in this chapter you'll learn exactly what types of loans are available and which ones may be right for you. You'll also learn the wisest ways to pay your loans back (or get out of paying them back altogether).

6. **The State System**

   State tuition, state scholarships—don't underestimate the treasures your state can offer you. In this chapter you'll learn how your own home state might wind up being your best friend when it comes to paying for college.

7. **The Other Aid**

   If you study hard in high school, you can potentially save thousands of dollars in tuition—this chapter will tell you how. And paying for college doesn't stop once you're finally at the college gates. You'll also find out how you can keep earning money for college—or get out of paying tuition—by taking advantage of campus resources such as internships and work-study.

8. **The Offer**

   The financial aid offer you receive isn't set in stone, and this chapter will tell you how to understand what you've been given—and how to get more.

9. **The Long Haul**

   Applying for financial aid isn't a one-time thing, and this chapter will give you tips on how to maximize your financial aid *every* year you're in school.

10. **The Secrets**

    From how to get extra money in the summer to how to combine strategies to hit your financial aid outta the park, this chapter will give you insider tips and secrets on how to *really* pay for college.

Before we get started, take a look at these 10 questions to see how much you really know about paying for college. The answers follow.

1 You've gotten into college, it costs way more than you can afford, and you don't have the grades or the athletic ability to win a free ride. What do you do?

   A. Something will work out. It always does. Patience is a virtue.

   B. Learn Origami. Your drum-playing certainly won't win you any scholarships, and you don't have time to learn anything else.

   C. Accept your fate. No way will any college give money to a B student. Time to pay the price for all those nights of instant messaging.

   D. Fill out the right financial aid forms—you can pay for college with need-based aid.

2 A great long-term plan for paying for college includes which of the following types of housing?

   A. Your grandparents' garage. It's not very cozy, but your grandmother will cook, and your parents can put all their spare cash in a savings account earmarked for college.

   B. The sleeping car of an Amtrak train. All your parents' get-rich-quick schemes involve a lot of disguises and moving around.

   C. A rented apartment very, very close to Harvard's campus. The sheer proximity will be good luck, even if the apartment is pretty shabby.

   D. A house your parents own themselves. Owning a home can actually help your parents pay for college.

3 Your local community college looks pleasant enough, with a nice campus and a decent library. But you want to go to college. This isn't the place for an ambitious student like you. Or is it?

   A. Sure it is. You secretly hate school. Community college is an easy way out.

   B. Definitely not. Last year there was this rumor in town that all the students at the community college were ex-cons. Seriously—it was in the paper. Oh, wait, no it wasn't. It was an email chain message. But still.

   C. Um, no. You're smart.

   D. It's an option. Cheaper tuition, the ability to transfer to a four-year school, and skilled professors make this a pretty decent choice if your financial aid possibilities aren't looking good.

4 You requested a scholarship brochure from the college you're applying to, but you don't think you're qualified for anything. But, you know you can't give up so easily. Could the college still have some free money they're not telling you about?

   A. No. Go ahead and buy some new shoes to ease the disappointment.
   B. Yes. Everyone has it out for you. At least your conspiracy theory is gaining credibility.
   C. No, and don't go asking around. Nobody likes meddling kids.
   D. Probably. In fact, many tuition waivers are never listed in any printed material.

5 The financial aid office has informed you that you have been awarded a $1,000 subsidized Stafford loan and a $2,000 unsubsidized Stafford loan. You need only $500, though, to make ends meet. What should you do?

   A. That extra $2,500 will be useful for something—take it all.
   B. Don't be greedy. Take the larger unsubsidized loan and decline the smaller subsidized loan. Congratulate yourself for being both wise and thrifty.
   C. You might need only $500, but who turns down extra money? You don't really have to repay a subsidized loan anyway, right?
   D. If $500 is all you need, then consider declining everything except for $500 of subsidized Stafford loan. You can always ask for more later on.

6 The financial aid office informed you that you might be eligible for a vocational scholarship, depending on your field of study. Is this something you should consider?

   A. Absolutely not! Vocation is just another word for work. The point of college is to avoid work.
   B. Wait a second! How does the financial aid office know what you're studying? This is getting creepier and creepier.
   C. Maybe—if you were one of those students who aspires to a "real" job. You just want to read—and dream—and dance!
   D. Definitely. If you know what you want to study and there's free money to help you do so, don't pass up the opportunity.

7   Your parents think that working a few hours per week during college through work-study will be a good way of paying for college. You, on the other hand, are concerned that your earnings will reduce your chances of receiving another Pell Grant. Who's correct?

A. Wait a second. Work-study? What is that, an oxymoron?

B. You're correct. You obviously know that dependent student earnings count much higher against you than parental earnings. Let them do the working—you've got class.

C. Both you and your parents are sort of correct. You might lose your Pell Grant, but hard work builds character.

D. Your parents are correct. Earnings from work-study jobs, unlike earnings from other kinds of jobs, will not adversely impact your EFC.

8   You have additional expenses that you don't think are adequately addressed in your financial aid award letter and that you'd like the financial aid office to consider. But you've also heard that colleges only rarely approve student appeals. Should you just accept what they've offered?

A. Yes. Better to just sit quietly—surely the college knew what it was doing when it calculated your award. Who are you to challenge it?

B. Yes. The tougher and more expensive college is, the more you'll appreciate it once you've paid off your student loans in thirty years.

C. Yes. Accept the offer, but consider an appeal later on once you've cashed in your financial aid.

D. No. Actually, financial aid appeals are approved in nearly one out of every two cases. If you have a legitimate reason for why you should get more aid and can back it up, the effort may be well worth the trouble.

9   Unfortunately, your first semester was a bust. You were failing every class, so you decided to drop out. You're now on academic probation and ineligible for financial aid until you get your grades back up and repay part of your Pell Grant. Can you simply start all over at a new college and leave this little mess behind?

A. Yes. That's a great idea. You'll be a more interesting person now that you have a few skeletons in your closet.

B. Sure. Society will cut you some slack. When you think about it, you're still just a teenager. Nobody really expects you to be responsible yet.

C. Maybe. But be sure to grow a beard and start going by the nickname "Scooter," just in case they somehow track you down.

D. Unfortunately, no. It's far better to face your problems now. Even if you reenroll at a new college, you won't be able to get financial aid.

10 You read that a great work-study position will be available over the
    summer in the biology department. But since you didn't receive work-
    study during the academic year, is there any hope you might get it over
    the summer?

    A. No chance. But with any luck, you'll find the next best thing: a job deliv-
    ering pizzas to the biology department.

    B. No. And don't even bother asking the financial aid office. You're starting
    to get sick of that "sorry, wish we could help you" look.

    C. Maybe. Just as there's "hope" that you'll win the lottery.

    D. Yes. Second chances and the occasional miracle do exist in financial aid.

Answers

1

Answer: D. Most financial aid is based on your financial need. If you can't afford to pay all of the tuition and fees, need-based aid will help you out through loans, grants, and other assistance. Your grades and (question-able) talents won't affect your eligibility for need-based aid. **See Chapter 1.**

2

Answer: D. The institutional methodology considers home equity when evaluating your ability to pay for college. If you're applying to schools that use this method, your parents can take out a home equity loan, which is a line of credit that is secured against the value of your home. A home equity loan can make their assets appear smaller, which can lower your EFC. **See Chapter 7.**

3

Answer: D. Many students are drawn to the low cost and flexibility of a community college. You might be surprised by the caliber of students who choose to begin their college education here. Don't rule it out too quickly. **See Chapter 3.**

4

Answer: D. Although scholarships at colleges are typically well-publicized, financial aid and admissions offices often have access to administrative pools of money that they can use to leverage student enrollment. Regardless of what the brochures say, some free money may still be available. **See Chapter 4.**

5

Answer: D. Subsidized loans are more favorable than unsubsidized loans, since the government will pay any accrued interest while you are enrolled in college at least half-time. You should borrow as little as possible to cover your needs, especially since you can ask the financial aid office to reinstate any Stafford loan money you previously declined if you turn out to need it after all. **See Chapter 5.**

6

Answer: D. Many states have financial aid set aside for certain fields of study, or for students enrolled in vocational-technical programs. In a few cases, however, if you don't earn the degree for which you've received assistance, you might be required to repay those funds. Common fields of study supported by state aid include teaching, medicine, and fire/police services. **See Chapter 6.**

7

Answer: D. As much as it may pain you, your parents still know a thing or two. Work-study earnings are exempt from the federal methodology formula that calculates your EFC. Although it does count as a resource, it in no way reduces your eligibility for need-based financial aid. **See Chapter 7.**

8

Answer: D. A National Association of Student Financial Aid Administrators survey found that 48 percent of student appeals led to an increase in financial aid. However, you should act quickly in order to have the best shot of winning the limited financial aid that's available. **See Chapter 8.**

9

Answer: D. All colleges that participate in federal financial aid programs communicate through a national database known as NSLDS. You'll be unable to receive any more federal financial aid until you settle your repayment and academic progress issues. **See Chapter 9.**

10

Answer: D. Even if you didn't receive work-study during the regular academic year, you might still receive an award during the summer. In fact, your chances might be pretty good since far fewer students attend college during the summer. **See Chapter 10.**

1

THE PROCESS

How much does college cost?
Imagine buying a brand new Lexus
every year for the next four years.

Common Acronyms

1

COA: Cost of Attendance

2

EFC: Expected Family Contribution

3

FAFSA: Free Application for Federal Student Aid

4

SAR: Student Aid Report

5

SEOG: Supplemental Educational
Opportunity Grant

6

SAP: Satisfactory Academic Progress

7

FWS: Federal Work Study Program

8

PLUS: Parent Loan for Undergraduate Students

9

FAA: Financial Aid Administrator

10

PJ: Professional Judgment

On Your Mark . . .

Financial aid is a competition. Thousands of students apply for the same money each year, and, unfortunately, college financial aid officers may not always give you the full story. You need to level the playing field.

Get Set . . .

For you, leveling the playing field means, first and foremost, understanding the terminology of financial aid. Financial aid officers use lots of obscure terms that don't always mean what you'd *think* they mean. To get ahead in the process you need to know what the people behind the financial aid desk are *really* saying.

Lingo!

During the application process, you'll encounter a seemingly endless string of terms and phrases. Don't panic. Despite all the obscure terms financial aid administrators may throw at you, they really want to know just one thing: how needy are you?

Your initial working vocabulary needs to include the most common sources and types of financial aid. Financial aid officers have an uncanny ability to come up with new words and phrases daily, so unless you're on a steady IV drip of gingko biloba, don't try to memorize all this at once.

Need

The Department of Education defines *need* as the difference between how much college costs and how much you can actually pay for it. In financial aid-speak, *need* is the difference between your Cost of Attendance (COA) and your Expected Family Contribution (EFC). If your college costs are greater than your ability to pay, then you have need. Financial aid officers figure out your level of need by using a process known as *needs analysis.*

Most financial aid is based on need, so the needier you are, the better off you'll be. Sounds like the perfect formula for an unhealthy relationship.

Needs Analysis

Needs analysis is the method financial aid officers use to determine how much need-based aid you can receive. Remember: *need* is the difference between the college's Cost of Attendance and your Expected Family Contribution. The needs-analysis formula looks like this:

Cost of Attendance – Expected Family Contribution = Need

Let's get to the point. If your EFC is zero, then your need will be exactly equal to the COA. On the other hand, if your EFC is greater than your COA, then your need is zero. More likely, your EFC will be lower than the COA, and you'll have some degree of need.

Cost of Attendance (COA)

Remember: the higher the COA estimate, the better. A high COA means your need will appear even greater, which means you'll be eligible for more need-based aid.

When you think about the cost of college, you probably think about tuition. Tuition does make up most of the Cost of Attendance (COA) at a typical private college, but the opposite is true for many public colleges and universities, where the largest part of COA includes room and board. COA can also include transportation expenses, personal expenses, loan fees, and a reasonable amount for the one-time purchase of a computer.

The COA is not the same as a bill. The COA is the college's estimate of what your total costs will be for the year. Typically, the only part of that estimate for which you will be billed is tuition and fees, and room and board if you live in campus housing. The COA can be as much as $8,000 to $12,000 higher than your tuition. If you're great at living on a shoestring, you'll find your total cost to be below that estimate. Thrift store, anyone?

Ten Things COA can include:
1. Fees and books
2. Living expenses
3. Meals
4. Transportation
5. Personal expenses

6. Dependent care
7. Computer purchase
8. Costs related to a disability
9. Costs for eligible study-abroad program
10. Entertainment

Expected Family Contribution (EFC)

Your Expected Family Contribution (EFC) is what the government thinks you can pay for college. The EFC is calculated using the information you provide on the Free Application for Federal Student Aid (FAFSA).

Depending on how much you and your family have in financial assets and how accurately you completed the FAFSA, your EFC can be anywhere from $0 to $99,999. Your EFC, whatever the amount, is what the Department of Education thinks you and your family should have to pay for college out of your own pocket.

There's a good chance your EFC will feel too high, especially if you have very little cash but large amounts of savings or real estate investments. Don't panic—we'll tell you how to cover your EFC if you don't have the money on hand.

In the financial aid administrator's eyes, you really are just a number. Your goal is to be as small a number as possible, since the smaller your EFC, the greater chance you have of receiving need-based aid.

EFC Calculation Tables

For a quick estimate of what your EFC is likely to be, refer to the tables on the next page. However, a warning: tables like these are generally not that accurate, so don't despair if your EFC seems way too high. The actual federal methodology is so complicated that your real EFC is unlikely to come close to what you find on these tables. For a better estimate, consult one of the free online EFC calculators at **www.finaid.org**.

The following tables are based on a simple calculation of your income, family size, and assets. Remember: this gives only a rough estimate. Additional elements, such as your older parent's age, your state of residence, and a host of other factors, such as child support and IRA savings, will impact your actual EFC. The following tables assume parental assets of $20,000. Remember that student assets count against you at a much higher rate.

Notice how having an additional student in college substantially decreases your EFC—nearly in half. Family size, however, has less of an impact on your EFC the higher your family income.

One in College			
Family Size	5	4	3
Income			
$20,000	0	0	0
$40,000	$1,200	$2,000	$3,000
$60,000	$6,100	$7,800	$9,700
$80,000	$14,400	$16,000	$18,000
$100,000	$23,200	$25,000	$27,000

Two in College			
Family Size	5	4	3
Income			
$20,000	0	0	0
$40,000	$800	$1,200	$1,700
$60,000	$3,500	$4,400	$5,400
$80,000	$7,700	$8,600	$9,600
$100,000	$12,000	$13,000	$14,000

Need-Based Aid

The amount of need-based aid you get depends only on how much need you have. Your grades, activities, and general fabulousness are not factors. Your need-based aid will be limited to the COA minus your EFC. The higher the COA, the more need you'll have.

Need-based aid can include:

- Pell Grants
- Supplemental Educational Opportunity Grants (SEOG)
- Perkins loans
- Most college work-study
- Most state grants
- The subsidized portion of the Stafford loan
- Scholarships and tuition waivers

For many students, especially those attending public institutions, receiving a full award consisting of need-based aid will cover most of the costs of attending college.

Nonneed-Based Aid

Just because the financial aid office has estimated your EFC to be $10,000 doesn't mean you have $10,000 on hand to use for college. In fact, you might be wondering how, exactly, you're supposed to come up with that money. Not to worry: nonneed-based aid can help you cover the amount of your EFC.

Nonneed-based aid includes awards, scholarships, and tuition waivers that are based on merit or other factors, including academics, athletics, musical talents, and enrollment leveraging. Federal sources of nonneed-based aid include unsubsidized Stafford loans and Parent Loans for Undergraduate Students (PLUS). Though helpful, these are actually the least favorable forms of government aid, with stricter repayment policies than the Perkins loan and subsidized Stafford loans. The PLUS loan also has a higher interest rate than the Perkins loan and both kinds of Stafford loans.

Though the interest rates for unsubsidized and subsidized Stafford loans are the same, interest for the unsubsidized Stafford loan starts accruing while you're still in school. The subsidized Stafford loan doesn't start accruing interest until six months after you graduate.

FEDERAL
Aid Limits

1
Pell Grant: $4,050

2
SEOG: $4,000

3
Perkins loan: $4,000

4
PLUS loan: Up to COA, minus other aid

5
Work-study: Usually a maximum of 20 hours per week

6
Stafford loan, freshman year: $2,625

7
Stafford loan, sophomore year: $3,500

8
Stafford loan, junior and senior years: $5,500

9
Additional unsubsidized Stafford loan:
Freshman and sophomore years: $4,000

10
Additional unsubsidized Stafford loan:
Junior and senior years: $5,000

The Methods

Plenty of madness reigns in the methods used to compute your EFC and, ultimately, your need. You can take advantage of this madness to raise your costs, lower your EFC, and increase your aid, but first, you need to know how financial aid administrators come up with these numbers.

The Federal Way

The primary method of determining your EFC is the one used by the Department of Education in the Free Application for Federal Student Aid, known affectionately by millions of students nationwide as the FAFSA. The FAFSA will require you to provide personal information, such as family size, marital or dependent status, income, and assets. An organization known as the Federal Processor then calculates your level of eligibility for financial aid. The formula used by the Federal Processor is known as the "federal methodology." Life would be simple if this were the only formula used by colleges to calculate your student financial aid package. Unfortunately, this is often not the case.

The Institutional Way

Many schools require you to submit other applications in addition to the FAFSA. More than 600 schools, for example, use the CSS/Financial Aid PROFILE form to determine students' eligibility for nonfederal financial aid. Plus, colleges usually have their own financial aid forms and make their calculations using the "institutional methodology." A college's institutional methodology is often stricter than the federal methodology, taking into account not only your financial assets but also the value of any property you or your family may own, including your home, which the FAFSA does not do.

The FAFSA Form

True mastery of the financial aid application process begins with an understanding of the FAFSA form. The FAFSA is your typical federal form: a lumbering, flawed giant filled with threatening and confusing language. Many students don't apply for aid because they think the form is too complicated, too imposing, or too unfair, and many families don't complete the FAFSA because they believe they're too wealthy to qualify for aid. Both of these decisions are almost always mistakes. Don't let the form intimidate you. It's become easier to complete in recent years, with more free, online resources than ever before.

10 Things About the FAFSA

Though the intent of this book is not to provide a line-by-line analysis of the FAFSA, there are 10 basic things about the FAFSA you should know.

1. Prior Year Calculation

The FAFSA's method of needs analysis relies upon income from the year *before* you actually enroll in college. This prior year's income method means that the amount of financial aid you receive *this* year is based on what you and your family earned *last* year. In fact, the questions on the FAFSA will ask that you report the information directly from your family's previous year's Federal Income Tax return, including your Adjusted Gross Income, Number of Dependents, Income Tax, and Income Earned.

Bottom line: your strategy for maximizing your eligibility on the FAFSA begins in your junior year of high school. This all-important year is called the *base income year.*

2. "As of Today"

On the FAFSA, you'll answer questions based on the prior year's earnings, with one exception: the "as of today" questions. The form will ask you to report, "as of today," your cash and savings on hand, the net value of your investments, and the net value of any business or farm your family owns. "As of today," as common sense dictates, means the date you complete and submit your FAFSA.

Without a doubt, a lightbulb in your head is filling the room with blinding effervescence right now: surely you understand the flaw with this request. In very simple terms, "as of today" means if tomorrow is payday, then your EFC will actually increase if you wait until tomorrow to complete the FAFSA. Tomorrow you'll have more cash on hand, which you'll need to report to the Federal Processor. Timing is everything.

3. Your Assets

The formula the FAFSA uses to calculate your EFC does not consider your parents' income the same as what you earn. In fact, assets in your name increase your EFC significantly more than do assets that belong to your parents. When the federal methodology calculates EFC, it assesses your parents' assets at less than 6 percent. Student assets, however, are assessed six times higher, around 35 percent. That means that 6 percent of your parents' assets and 35 percent of your own assets will, in theory, be used to pay for college. This difference can have huge implications on how much need-based aid you receive.

The bottom line: your parents have to give fewer of their assets than you do. The fewer assets students have, the better. Ever think you'd hear *that?*

It might sound crazy, but if you can afford not to work between your junior and senior years of high school, you shouldn't. If you do, you'll have to report it on the FAFSA, and your earnings could potentially raise your EFC and lessen the amount of aid you can receive.

Financial aid applicants who find out about this chink in the process after they have already completed the FAFSA are subject to fits of rage. If at any point you decide to share your newfound secrets with them, make sure you do so at a safe distance.

4. Your Parents' Assets

The FAFSA calculates parental income and assets at 6 percent, far below the 35 percent used to calculate the student's assets. The reason is fairly simple. The Department of Education realizes that for every dollar your parents earn, most of that money must go toward providing housing, food, and other family necessities. The FAFSA thinks no more than about 6 percent of parental assets should be reserved for covering the costs of their child's education.

5. Number of Family Members in College

The federal methodology divides the EFC by the number of students within a family who are attending college. The more students attending college at the same time, the more financial aid eligibility each one will have.

It might be too late to convince your parents to go for those quintuplets they've always dreamed about, but it might be a good time for that older sibling of yours to reenroll in college when you do if he or she has dropped out due to financial hardship. Do note, however, that parents enrolled in school, even full-time, don't count toward the number of family members currently in college. This benefit applies only to dependent children.

6. The Worksheets

To increase your potential for aid, you should almost never hold any savings in your own name. The loss of financial aid eligibility is just too great a risk.

When completing the FAFSA, don't overlook the section of the form known as the worksheets. For 2004–2005, there are three worksheets—A, B, and C—with separate columns for student and parent information. Worksheets A and B are known as income inclusion formulas, which increase your EFC. Worksheet C is an income exclusion formula, and amounts listed in this worksheet reduce your EFC.

You'll need to understand the differences in the worksheets when you start considering short-term and long-term strategies for receiving more aid. Making mistakes in your answers can hurt your eligibility. (More on the worksheets in Chapter 2, "The Long Plan," and Chapter 3, "The Short Plan.")

You should file the FAFSA as early as possible after January 1 every year, regardless of when you plan on filing your taxes. Federal aid is limited—don't miss out!

7. Tax Returns

The information you provide on the FAFSA, such as your income and asset amounts, will come directly from your tax return. Since the FAFSA is due before you submit your taxes, however, you're permitted to estimate the numbers.

Don't wait to file your FAFSA until after you've filed your tax return—waiting is a mistake. The FAFSA makes clear that you can estimate, and it's perfectly understandable that the amounts may not be exact. You should try to make accurate estimates, but don't be afraid to guess in your favor. You certainly don't want to overestimate your income and assets and reduce the amount of aid you might otherwise receive.

8. Selected for Verification

The financial aid office might ask you to submit copies of your and your parents' federal tax returns in order to confirm that what you submitted on the FAFSA is accurate. This process, known as *verification*, is the Department of Education's method of reducing fraud. If you are selected for verification, don't panic—you didn't do anything wrong (even if the financial aid officer always seems to give you a sideways glance when you stroll into the office). This isn't a punishment. Verification is often based on a certain percentage of randomly selected files. At some schools, 100 percent of all enrolled students are "selected" for verification.

To complete the verification process, follow the instructions the financial aid office gives you as quickly as possible to avoid losing out on limited aid.

Don't be afraid to call or email the financial aid office to check on your application. Most larger colleges don't have the staff to personally call you when you've been selected for verification or if parts of your forms are incomplete. Instead, they rely on standard mail service to deliver a form letter to your permanent home address. Keep checking until you are absolutely sure your file is complete.

9. The Zero EFC

Parents with a combined adjusted gross income or earned income of $15,000 or less, and who are not required to file a 1040 long form, qualify for an automatic zero EFC. Having a zero EFC means that you are eligible to receive the most favorable financial aid package.

10. Student Aid Report (SAR)

Once you've completed and submitted the FAFSA, the Department of Education will calculate your EFC and send it to you in a Student Aid Report (SAR). If you completed the hard copy of the FAFSA, a paper version of the

Families who have an adjusted gross income of less than $50,000 can submit a short form of the 1040, either the 1040EZ or 1040A. Submitting one of the short forms enables you to undergo a more favorable needs analysis known as the simplified needs test. This method of calculating EFC disregards assets, making the student eligible for more aid.

SAR will arrive in the mail anywhere from four to six weeks after submission. If you filed electronically at www.fafsa. ed.gov, you'll be able to download an electronic copy of your SAR as soon as two weeks after filing.

Because the SAR provides you with your EFC, it's important to receive this information as soon as possible. Your EFC tells you whether or not you're eligible for certain kinds of financial aid, such as the Pell Grant, and it's also the number that will help determine your overall need.

Time is of the essence, so we recommend filing your FAFSA electronically, if possible. It's free, it's much faster than filing a paper FAFSA, and it's a great opportunity to visit one of the few websites left with virtually no pop-ups.

To file your FAFSA and get your SAR online, you'll need to provide an electronic signature by registering for a Personal Identification Number (PIN). You'll find information on how to do this on the website, www.fafsa.ed.gov.

The Pesky Profile

In addition to requiring the FAFSA, many schools ask students to complete an additional form known as the College Scholarship Services (CSS)/Financial Aid PROFILE Application. Colleges requiring this form often explain to their students that the FAFSA's needs analysis is too simple to paint an accurate picture of a family's ability to pay for their child's education.

As your intuition may be telling you, when a college has to explain its reasons for a policy, that policy is usually tied to more dollars out of your pocket.

You have to pay a fee to complete the PROFILE—the little Visa logo on the PROFILE website probably gave that away. The PROFILE is also tougher than the FAFSA: it takes into account assets that the FAFSA leaves alone, such as the equity in the parents' primary residence, which often means you qualify for less aid. Although the strategies of this guide are primarily concerned with the FAFSA and the federal methodology, we'll give you some advice later on regarding the PROFILE.

The Deadlines

One last word before going into more detail about how to pay for college. By far, the single greatest reason most students miss out on financial aid is that they wait to file the forms or fail to submit corrections in a timely manner. Getting financial aid, as we've said before, is a competition, and speed counts. In the eyes of the computer that processes your paperwork, the number that sometimes matters most is the date you submit a complete application.

Each school will have unique deadlines for both federal and institutional aid, including unique deadlines for individual scholarships. It's in your best interest to complete each form at the absolute earliest date possible, even if you must estimate financial figures.

The FAFSA form becomes available after January 1 every year, and you can't complete or submit it prior to this date. This means that if you're planning to enroll in August 2005, the FAFSA itself will not become available until January 2005. This is quite different from many scholarship applications, which are often due up to ten months before classes begin.

Onward

With your brand-new vocabulary and basic understanding of the process, you're ready to uncover the secrets of financial aid success. In the next nine chapters, we'll give you some great strategies to help you master the game.

"The one piece of advice we try to pass on to all students is to complete your financial aid paperwork as soon as possible. The longer you wait, the more likely it is you'll miss out on financial assistance."

**Whitney
Financial Aid
Administrator**

Simplified Needs Checklist

If you don't have to report any of the following ten items on a 1040 long form, you may be eligible to file either the 1040A or 1040EZ. See your accountant for more information.

1

Taxable refunds or credits of local or state taxes

2

Alimony received or paid

3

Capital gain or loss

4

Rent, real estate, royalties, partnerships, S corporations, or trusts

5

Business Income

6

Farm income

7

Keogh retirement/SEP deduction

8

Taxable income more than $50,000

9

Self-employment tax

10

Tax on IRAs and other retirement plans

2

THE LONG PLAN

"I am too big to climb and play," said the boy. "I want to buy things and have fun. I want some money. Can you give me some money?"

Shel Silverstein
The Giving Tree

Ever hear the fable about the ant and the grasshopper? The grasshopper lazes away the summer while the ant works hard every day, thinking about the future. The ant comes out on top during the long, cold winter, while the grasshopper winds up decorating the ant's lawn as an ice sculpture. Or something like that.

You, of course, are the ant, planning for the future and saving for college. Is Uncle Sam really going to foot the entire bill? He does, after all, have around 20 million nieces and nephews. Time to talk about a long-term plan to pay for college.

Long-Term *Thinking*

A long-term plan for paying for college involves more than just racking up investments and accruing savings. There are other things you and your parents need to think about. In just about every area, the earlier you start thinking about college, the better off you'll be.

Scholastics

Your number-one asset when it comes to paying for college is your approach to school. If college is still three or more years away, your long plan has to include strategies that will help you improve your grades, diversify your activities and volunteerism, and identify the scholarships that will help you pay for your education.

Don't think of scholarships as a short-term strategy. The truth is that you can "win" many scholarships years before you even apply for them. Every hour of community service and every tenth of a grade point you earn as a freshman, sophomore, and junior in high school count toward potential scholarship money. We'll discuss strategies for winning scholarships in Chapter 4, "The Free Money."

Family Matters

When two or more siblings are in college at the same time, the amount of financial aid available to you can increase considerably. The federal needs-analysis formula divides your EFC by the number of children from your family attending college simultaneously. Some families decide when to have a second or third child, or when to adopt, as a part of their long-term college planning. This is a highly personal choice and is obviously not applicable for every family—but it's one more thing to keep in mind.

Retirement

Too many parents sacrifice their own retirement plans to pay for their children's college educations. Money may indeed be tighter once you start college, but your parents shouldn't decrease their Individual Retirement Accounts (IRAs) or other retirement contributions. You might even get more aid if your parents *increase* contributions to their retirement plans.

Your parents should plan for their retirement just as vigorously as they plan how to pay for your college education. If they don't, in the long, long term they'll be worse off, and you and your siblings will need to support them through their retirement years. If your parents have to choose between saving for your college education and saving for their retirement, consider these ten factors:

1. College savings plans are considered in the federal needs-analysis formula.

2. Retirement savings are exempt from the federal needs-analysis formula.

3. College savings are typically restricted to use only in paying for qualified educational expenses.

4. Retirement savings may be used for any needed expenses upon retirement.

5. College savings come with tax benefits, some of which are set to expire in the next five to ten years.

6. Retirement savings come with tax benefits that have no expiration date.

7. College savings may be supplemented by federally guaranteed student loans, if insufficient.

8. Insufficient retirement savings necessitate making difficult choices that affect quality of life.

Most colleges won't take retirement savings into consideration when calculating your EFC. If your parents contribute money to 401K plans, IRAs, and some other types of retirement accounts, they can shelter their assets, qualify for more financial aid, and protect their futures.

Since 529 plans are now available nationwide, you're only a phone call or mouse click away from finding the one in your state. Contact the College Savings Plans Network (CSPN) either through its website, **www. collegesavings. org**, or its toll-free number, 1-877-277-6496.

9. College savings will help you survive four or five years of college.

10. Retirement savings will help your parents survive the rest of their lives.

A Note About Our Goal

It's possible that your family may be considered too well-off financially to qualify for much need-based aid. If that's true, your need-based aid is often limited to Stafford loans. In fact, fewer than 4 percent of families with incomes of more than $60,000 qualify for the Pell Grant, and these families typically have unusual circumstances, such as four or more children in college at once or high medical expenses. In this book, our goal is to help you maximize your need-based aid. Families who know they won't be eligible for need-based aid will want to save differently for college.

The 529 Plans

Ever wish you could go back in time and pay for college when tuition was affordable? All you need to do is invent a time machine—and your college-cost worries are over. Get cracking, Einstein.

In the meantime, you actually *can* lock in today's tuition rates and avoid the annual increase in costs. Known as Section 529 plans, they essentially allow you and your family to pay now toward your future tuition. As of 2002, every state, plus the District of Columbia, has a Section 529 plan. "Section 529" refers to the corresponding part of the Internal Revenue Code. Any 529 plan must be part of a long-term strategy since it takes time for money to accrue. The earlier you start saving money through a 529, the better.

There are two kinds of 529 plans: prepaid tuition plans and college savings plans.

Prepaid Tuition Plans

Prepaid tuition plans allow you and your parents to pay for college *now*, at current costs, rather than waiting and facing skyrocketing prices. A prepaid tuition plan guarantees that if you buy four years' worth of tuition right now, at current costs, you'll be able to attend four years of college later on without having to pay the increased cost of tuition. This is a significant savings. In the past decade, private college tuition has risen 42 percent and public college tuition 47 percent, and will likely rise, on average, 5 percent each year for the next decade.

When you redeem the tuition credits you've purchased, their maximum value depends on the average tuition of in-state public colleges. If you decide to go to either an in-state private college or an out-of-state college, you can usually apply the tuition you've bought toward that college's tuition. However, you'll have to make up the difference between the value of the average public college's tuition and the cost for tuition at the private or out-of-state college. The exact details of these plans vary from state to state.

Though prepaid tuition plans are a great deal in some ways, you'll see in just a moment how they can adversely affect your chances for need-based aid.

The College Savings Plan

A 529 college savings plan allows you, your parents, or anyone else to contribute to the future costs of college and get some tax benefits in the process. Unlike the prepaid tuition plans, the college savings plans don't come with any guarantee on returns. Like regular investments in the stock market, there is a chance that you could actually lose the money you've invested in them.

College savings plans often allow contributors to choose how their money is invested. Options include higher-risk equity funds for potential long-term growth or safer fixed-income investments when college is fewer than five years down the road.

If your 529 account ever needs to be transferred, such as if you decide not to attend college, you can transfer your account to your:

- Spouse
- Daughter/son
- Stepdaughter/ stepson
- Sister/brother
- Stepsister/ stepbrother
- Mother/father
- Stepmother/ stepfather
- Niece/nephew
- Aunt/uncle
- First cousin

Whereas you can use the prepaid tuition plan only for tuition and mandatory fees, you can use college savings plans for any COA expenses, including room, board, books, and supplies.

Who Can Use the Plans?

The 529 plans are great for families whose only other aid would be in the form of loans, for families who want to save money in a way that is currently tax-deferred and tax-free when the money is used for college, and especially for students who plan to attend an in-state public college several years down the road.

These plans are an even better option when a grandparent or relative other than a parent decides to open the account. Although the Department of Education may close this loophole in the future, currently the FAFSA considers 529 plans assets of the contributor (the person who puts money into the plans), not of the beneficiary (you). On the FAFSA, you have to report the assets held only by either you or your parents. You don't have to report a 529 plan held by a grandparent or other relative. As you recall, assets are anything you or your parents own of value (such as savings or real estate), and the fewer assets you report on the FAFSA, the lower your EFC will be. Your EFC needs to be as low as possible so you can get more financial aid.

Which Plan to Choose?

There are pros and cons to both kinds of 529 plans, and the one you choose, if you choose one at all, depends on your particular financial situation. For example, if your number-one concern is locking in current tuition rates and you're sure you're unlikely to receive need-based aid, the 529 prepaid tuition plan is the better option. That's because the 529 college savings plan does not come with a guarantee to cover the rise in tuition rates. On the other hand, if you feel as if you'll probably receive need-based aid, the 529 college savings plan is likely the better option, since it will not reduce your other aid (unlike the 529 prepaid tuition plan, which counts as a resource).

Other subtle differences between these plans, such as the ability to control your investment and the amount of flexibility in how your money is used for college expenses, will likewise help you determine which is the better option. By and large, however, the 529 college savings plan, because of its flexibility and lack of impact on your other financial aid, will likely prove to be the better choice.

529 Plan Pros

There are plenty of benefits to both kinds of 529 plans.

Tax Benefits

The prepaid tuition plan and the college savings plan both have tax benefits. Through the year 2010, amounts used from 529 plans grow tax-deferred and are exempt from federal taxes if you use the amounts for qualified educational expenses. In addition, many states offer state-tax exemptions or deductions, making the plans attractive options for a more general savings strategy. "Tax-deferred" simply means that you owe no federal taxes on the interest that grows from your savings until you actually cash it in. "Tax-exempt" means that you never have to pay taxes on the interest you earn from your savings.

Some states offer better tax savings than others, and some states offer substantial savings. Strategy is key here. For example, if you find that your state limits your state tax deduction to $2,000, you can get around this limit by creating not one but several 529 accounts for an individual student, thus increasing the total amount of taxes you can deduct. Tricky!

There are two kinds of 529 plans, and each is slightly different. For example, the 529 prepaid tuition plan actually counts as a financial aid resource, which could reduce your other financial aid. The 529 college savings plan does not count as a financial aid resource. If you decide to invest in a 529 plan, make sure you understand the rules of each type.

10

THINGS
About 529s

The Prepaid Tuition Plan:

1

Guarantees that the amount you save will cover tuition increases

2

May reduce eligibility for need-based aid

3

Gives no choice in how your money is invested

4

Is offered in fewer states than the college savings plan

5

May be limited to specific, in-state colleges

The College Savings Plan:

6

Is not counted as a financial aid resource

7

May be used for any COA expense

8

Has flexibility and choice in how your money is invested

9

Has no limits to how you can use the funds

10

Has no guarantee that your investment will cover tuition increases

Control

The 529 college savings plans allow you some choice in how your money is invested. If college is many years away, your parents may want to invest in more aggressive funds with a higher potential for return. You can even change this option once every calendar year.

If your parents are the account owners and you decide not to go to college, or if you win a full scholarship, your parents can transfer both types of 529 plans to another family member, even first cousins. Or they can hold on to them in case you decide to go to graduate school later on. Some prepaid tuition plans have restrictions in this regard, so check the plan in your state for details.

If you want to open either kind of 529 plan for someone else, you don't even have to be related to that person. Typically, parents are most likely to open 529 accounts, but grandparents, uncles, aunts, and even friends may do so as well. Time to update your Christmas list, yes?

A 2002 survey by Morgan Stanley found that more than half of families intending to send their children to college had not started saving at all. For those families who had started saving, 70 percent had started before their child's fifth birthday.

Tax-Free Gifts

Ever hear of the IRS "gift tax"? Individuals are typically allowed to give up to $11,000 each year to someone else tax-free. The 529 legislation, however, allows individuals to accelerate five years' worth of giving all at once. This means that your grandparents can open a 529 college savings plan for you with an initial investment of $55,000—tax-free. In terms of long-term planning, this is a great benefit: you stand to earn more in interest than if you were to invest only $11,000 each year for five years.

No Limits

Both prepaid tuition plans and college savings plans have fewer limits than other similar college savings programs. Unlike savings bonds or Coverdell Educational Savings Accounts, 529 plans have no income limitations. If you

GOOD THINGS
About the 529 Plan

1

Earnings grow tax-deferred.

2

Distributions are tax-exempt when used for college costs.

3

Accounts benefit from state-tax exemptions or deductions.

4

You can open 529 accounts for both relatives and friends.

5

You can choose how your money is invested in a 529 college savings plan.

6

Accounts can be transferred to other family members.

7

Accounts can be refunded, albeit with penalties.

8

There are no income limitations for who can open a 529 plan.

9

IRS gift-tax rules offer an accelerated giving benefit.

10

You have fewer time limits for use than other college savings plans.

win the lottery but still want to pay for college using this strategy, then 529 plans are just your thing.

The 529 college savings plans, in particular, also allow an extended period of time for usage. They are currently a popular choice among working parents who feel they may want to return to school at some point in the future. Both types of 529 plans can be established for parents as well as children.

Refunds

Should the need arise, you can request a refund of either kind of 529 plan. However, you'll have to pay a minimum penalty of 10 percent for doing so, in addition to other fees the various state plans may charge and an assessment of federal taxes on any of the refund not used for educational expenses. Still, you have the option.

529 Plan Cons

No plan is perfect, and there are some things you need to know about 529 plans before you rush out and cash in all your war bonds. These plans have very specific rules, and you should carefully study the plan you intend to use.

Fees and Costs

Most important, you should understand the fees and administrative costs of your state's 529 plans. If you're only two years away from college, and you're hoping to "freeze" current costs in order to save a thousand dollars or so, you might be unpleasantly surprised if the fees and costs from opening and maintaining your state's 529 plan wipe out any cost savings from annual tuition increases. In other words, unless you start early, the fees and costs of a 529 plan may outweigh the benefits.

Penalties

If the 529 prepaid tuition plan or college savings plan owner decides to withdraw the funds, he or she must pay a 10 percent fee, and any earnings are subject to federal taxation. Plus, since the money was invested on a tax-

BAD THINGS
About the 529 Plan

1

The 529 plan fees may make this a poor choice for short-term planning.

2

Withdrawing funds results in a 10 percent fee.

3

Funds for anything but school will be taxed.

4

Tax benefits are set to expire in 2011, barring legislation.

5

Prepaid tuition plans may reduce eligibility for other financial aid.

6

College savings plan accounts in your name will be assessed at
35 percent.

7

Prepaid tuition plan funds must be used within a limited time period.

8

Time extension may come with a penalty.

9

Funds can't be used for most foreign schools.

10

Funds can't be used for schools not considered "eligible institutions of
higher education."

deferred basis, it will be taxed if it is used for anything other than qualified educational expenses.

Limited Time

Some states stipulate that you must use 529 prepaid tuition plans within a fixed period of time. For example, some states require you to use them within ten years of your high school graduation. While you usually have some options for extending this time period, these options can come at a cost.

Limited Tax Benefits

Although 529 plans currently offer tax-exempt withdrawals from the college savings plan, this benefit isn't permanent. In 2011, both prepaid tuition plans and college savings plans will no longer be tax-free, unless Congress takes additional action. There's no way to know whether or not this tax benefit will remain. If you decide to invest in either the 529 prepaid tuition plan or college savings plan because of the tax benefits, you should understand that these benefits may no longer exist once you decide to go to school.

Limited Choices

Want to attend a foreign school, or a school that isn't considered an "eligible institution of higher education"? If so, you'll lose the tax benefits of a prepaid tuition plan or college savings plan. You may, in fact, have to request a refund in order to use the money—with a penalty, of course.

The prepaid tuition plan can be a very bad choice for someone who has a very low EFC and would otherwise qualify for a full range of need-based aid.

Financial Aid Impact

Though prepaid tuition plans and college savings plans are both good ways to save for college, they can negatively affect your chances for other financial aid.

THINGS

About the Coverdell ESA

Pros:

1

Unlimited investment options

2

Few limits placed on where funds may be used

3

May be set up at virtually any brokerage firm

4

No expiration date for Coverdell tax benefits

5

Tax-free withdrawals for qualified educational expenses

Cons:

6

A $2,000 annual contribution limit

7

Varying setup fees and other administrative costs

8

Income limitations on who may participate

9

Counted as a student asset in the needs-analysis formula, which greatly reduces other aid eligibility

10

Generally must be used before the student reaches thirty years of age

The 529 prepaid tuition plan counts as a financial aid resource, which means the college assumes it's available for you to use for college. For every dollar of prepaid tuition used, you'll see an equal reduction in the amount of potential financial aid available, with the exception of the Pell Grant. The prepaid tuition plan can be a very bad choice for someone who has a very low EFC and would otherwise qualify for a full range of need-based aid.

Money in the form of a college savings plan, however, is not counted as a resource but as an asset of the contributor. Since it's counted as an asset, it will be assessed at the usual rate of 6 percent if your parents own it and 35 percent if you do. This could increase your EFC. If your grandparents are the contributors, you'll be better off since the FAFSA doesn't ask you to report their assets.

The bottom line: both plans will reduce your need-based aid to some extent. But your aid will be reduced *less* with a college savings plan.

Coverdell ESAs

The Coverdell ESA (Education Savings Account), formerly known as the Education IRA, is another option for long-term college savings. These accounts are extremely flexible and offer marked advantages over the 529 plans. Of course, they also come with their own unique drawbacks.

Coverdell Pros

Coverdell ESAs give you virtually unlimited options for investments. Want to set something up at your current mutual-fund company? Coverdell ESAs will let you do just that.

Coverdell ESAs also allow tax-free withdrawals not only for college but also for private elementary or high schools. Another point for Coverdell.

Although contributions to both Coverdell ESAs and 529 plans are tax-exempt when used for educational expenses, the tax benefits for the Coverdell ESA aren't set to expire in 2011 as those for the 529 plans are. In this sense, Coverdell ESAs are a safer bet.

Coverdell Cons

The FAFSA considers Coverdell ESAs *your* asset, which means your account will be assessed at a rate of 35 percent. Again, like the 529, this can hurt your chances for need-based aid. If your family is eligible for need-based aid, you may want to avoid a Coverdell ESA.

The Coverdell ESA places a $2,000 annual limit on how much money can be contributed to one student. If your parent or grandparent exceeds this amount in any given year, the excess contribution is assessed at a 6 percent excise tax.

Single parents cannot contribute at all to the Coverdell ESAs if their modified adjusted gross incomes exceed $110,000. Couples whose combined adjusted gross income exceeds $220,000 also cannot contribute. The 529 plans have no such restrictions.

Other Savings Plans

Besides the 529 plans and Coverdell ESAs, and, of course, your own investments, you have two additional options for long-term college savings.

Custodial Accounts

If your parents really like living on the edge, they might opt for a custodial account. Also known as Uniform Gift to Minors Act (UGMA) accounts or Uniform Transfer to Minors Act (UTMA) accounts, these plans can be set up with just about any brokerage firm or mutual fund company and have some tax advantages. The main advantage has to do with the rate at which custodial account earnings are taxed. The first $750 is exempt, the next $750 is taxed at the child's lower federal rate, and anything beyond is taxed at the custodian's federal rate. In order to qualify for this benefit, you must be younger than fourteen.

Once you reach the age of majority, anywhere from eighteen to twenty-five depending on what state you live in, all funds within the account become your property. At this point, you're legally entitled to spend the money on anything you want—*not just college*. Of course, if your parents set up a custodial account to pay for college, you'll probably want to do just that. Your parents might view your freedom of choice as a risk they either are or are not willing to take.

•

Savings Bonds

Ah, yes, backed by the full faith and credit of the United States government, savings bonds have been around since 1935. Alas, like many things that have been around since 1935, savings bonds just don't seem as cool as all these new programs, with their fancy acronyms and code numbers. However, they do have many of the same benefits, including tax exemption, when used to cover the costs of education. And of course, the full faith and credit of the United States government never really goes out of style, does it?

Buying a Home

Owning a home can be one of the most effective ways to pay for college. The federal and institutional methodologies differ in how they treat the value of a home, and there are strategies you can apply to both systems to lower your EFC and maximize your aid.

The needs-analysis formula used by the FAFSA does not count the value of your family's primary home to calculate your EFC, though it does count savings and investments. Whether you live in a cardboard box or in a McMansion won't be a factor in calculating your EFC.

What does this mean for you and your family? If they can afford to, your parents should consider buying a home as part of their plan for paying for college. Since any money tied up in a home can't be touched by the federal methodology, your parents can actually protect their assets by investing in a home. In other words, owning a home actually reduces the appearance of your parents' assets, which can lower your EFC.

Treasury Direct

Although savings bonds may be old, that doesn't mean they're out of touch. In fact, the Department of the Treasury has set up a website that allows for easy online purchasing and management of Series EE and I savings bonds. Visit **www. savingsbonds. gov.**

10

THINGS

About Home Equity

1. Proceeds from a home equity loan, since it is cash on hand, will count as an asset. The amount of a line of credit will not. A line of credit works very much like a credit card, so it is not calculated at all when determining your EFC. If, however, you were to withdraw cash from your line of credit and deposit that cash into your checking account, you'd have to report that on your FAFSA.

2. The value of your primary residence is ignored by the FAFSA.

3. Interest is often fully tax deductible, unlike student or private loans, which at most offer partial tax credits.

4. Prepaying your mortgage, or switching to a fifteen-year mortgage, can often provide a greater long-term benefit than using the same money on a college savings plan.

5. The money from a home equity line of credit can be used for more than just tuition and fees.

6. There are no age limits or income restrictions to borrowing through a line of credit.

7. The home equity line of credit benefits are not set to expire.

8. Home equity funds can be used to pay down your other consumer debt, which is not considered in the needs-analysis formula.

9. Although interest rates are currently low, they are not limited by the federal government, as are student loans.

10. The market value of your home is considered by the needs analysis employed by many private colleges, potentially reducing the value of a home equity line of credit as a college payment strategy.

Home Equity Loans

Schools using the institutional methodology to determine your eligibility for their own financial aid often *will* include home equity in their calculations. Taking out a home equity loan actually *reduces* home equity—a good thing, in this case. When your parents borrow against the value of their home and reduce their home equity, they decrease their assets—and fewer assets can lead to a smaller EFC.

Your parents will pay interest only on the checks they actually draw against the loan, and interest paid on home equity loans is generally tax deductible. The equity needed to qualify for one of these loans typically takes several years of homeownership to build, which means you need to consider this as part of a long-term plan for paying for college.

The main drawback is that you must repay a home equity loan, unlike grants or scholarships. However, if your aid package consists of loans, and well over half of all financial aid comes in the form of loans, there is a very good chance that a home equity loan will come at a lower interest rate than the Stafford and PLUS Loans that make up most of today's educational borrowing.

The Long Haul

Wise planning and careful thinking can make all the difference when it comes to long-term planning for paying for college. The more time you have to save and invest, the better. Not everyone thinks so far ahead, however. Read on for tips on how to pay for college if you don't have years to get yourself in gear.

3

THE SHORT PLAN

"How did it get so late so soon?
It's night before it's afternoon.
December is here before it's June.
My goodness how the time has flewn.
How did it get so late so soon?"

Dr. Seuss

If you're like most people, there's a good chance you've put off this whole college planning thing until the last minute. Fortunately, all is not lost. Even if you're halfway through high school, there are some crucial short-term strategies that can save the day.

If you've been diligently saving since birth, read on nonetheless. For you, these short-term strategies will just be green-hued icing on the cake.

Tax Strategies

If imitation is the sincerest form of flattery, then the folks at the IRS must be very pleased to see how closely the FAFSA resembles the 1040 income tax form. How you and your parents fill out your tax forms makes all the difference in how much aid you receive. A short-term plan for paying for college focuses on minimizing the income and assets you report during the year *before* you start college.

Base Year

The federal needs analysis calculates your EFC by asking you to report your adjusted gross income from the *preceding tax year.* Financial aid officers will refer to this crucial year in several ways: prior year income, previous year income, or base year income. The *base year* is the period from January to December of the year *before* the opening semester or quarter of college. In other words, if your first year of college begins in September 2006, your base year would be January–December 2005.

To reduce your EFC and increase your financial aid, you must minimize your family's base year income. For example, if one of your parents receives a year-end bonus, postponing the bonus until the January before your freshman year of college will reduce the base year income. However, it will be included in EFC calculation for your sophomore year.

Simplified Needs Test

Parents who make around $50,000 should take a particularly close look at reducing income. The federal needs analysis includes a great benefit called the "simplified needs test" for any family with an income below this amount. The simplified needs test can significantly increase your aid eligibility since it ignores assets, such as cash and savings on hand. In order to qualify, combined parental income must be less than $50,000, and each family member must be eligible to file either the 1040EZ or 1040A form.

Before you convince your parents to leave their jobs and take an extended vacation, however, you should know that this simplified needs benefit applies only to the federal aid methodology. Private schools may still grant their own institutional aid based on your family's other assets, even if they did earn less than $50,000.

Education Tax Credits

In addition to minimizing income, you should also think about ways to increase your tax credits. The federal needs analysis allows you and your parents to exclude the amount of certain education credits from the base year. These credits include two programs that were created with the Taxpayer Relief Act of 1997: the Hope Credit and the Lifelong Learning Credit.

- A $1,500 Hope Credit: During your first two years of college, your parents will get a 100 percent tax credit for the initial $1,000 of your tuition and a 50 percent credit for the next $1,000. This credit is phased out for joint filers earning between $83,000 to $103,000, or single filers earning between $41,000 to $51,000.

- A $2,000 Lifelong Learning Credit: This amount represents a 20 percent tax credit for the first $10,000 of your tuition. There is no two-year limit, and your parents can claim this credit even when you go to graduate school. The same income levels as the Hope Scholarship apply.

You should find out if you and your parents qualify for these tax programs by reviewing IRS form 8863, available from **www.irs.gov**. Any amounts that you report on your federal tax return for Hope or Lifelong Learning Credits should be included on Worksheet C of your FAFSA.

Income Brackets

One of the main differences between the IRS and the Department of Education is their view of student income versus parent income. The IRS views individuals in terms of *brackets*, meaning that a student, at a lower tax

WAYS TO
Reduce Base Year Income

1

Postpone a year-end bonus to the next year.

2

Take an unpaid leave of absence.

3

Maximize contributions to retirement plans.

4

Try to have overtime payments deferred to the next year.

5

Don't earn more than $2,380 if you're a student.

6

Delay accepting large cash gifts.

7

Accelerate income, if possible, to the year before the base year.

8

Sell off losing investments.

9

Don't sell off real estate or stocks during the base year.

10

Pay down consumer debt.

bracket, should be assessed at a lower rate than the parent, who presumably earns more money and is in a higher bracket. For this reason, many financial advisors suggest putting more assets in the child's name, since less of this money will be lost to federal taxes.

This strategy does not work in the world of financial aid. The federal needs analysis views student and parent income differently. In the financial aid philosophy, student income is assessed more harshly because students typically do not need the majority of their earnings to pay for household needs, such as food and shelter. To maximize financial aid, your parents should *never* put assets in your name.

Income Protection

Your parents' income has an income protection as high as $29,000, meaning that only income above this amount is assessed for calculating EFC. The rate at which this income is assessed can be no higher than 47 percent and can be as low as 22 percent. In other words, the Department of Education expects that no family can possibly contribute more than half of their income toward college tuition. And depending on how much your parents earn, how many children they have in college, and a variety of other factors, the Department of Education may determine that no more than one quarter of your parents' income can be used for tuition. The FAFSA, in essence, tries to reserve, or protect, most of your parents' income for other expenses, such as housing and food.

Student income, on the other hand, has only a $2,380 protection, and anything a dependent student earns beyond this amount is assessed at 50 percent. In simple terms, for every two dollars you earn above $2,380, you lose one dollar in financial aid eligibility. What does this actually mean for you? *You're better off not working during the year before you enter college if you'll earn more than $2,380.*

"I worked and saved all summer, and in the end it wound up costing me financial aid! How did this happen?"

Andrew, 19

Income Penalty Exceptions

Behind every rule is an exception, and there are two exceptions regarding your income that may help you answer the age-old question: how can I earn money for college without being penalized in financial aid?

Work-Study

Work-study jobs are typically on-campus jobs with very flexible schedules that you can do during the semester, usually for a maximum of twenty hours per week. The money you earn from a work-study job is exempt from EFC calculation. No matter how much you earn in work-study, not one dollar of that amount will ever decrease your financial aid eligibility. In terms of federal needs analysis, it is as if you never worked a day the entire year and had an income of $0.

This free money should serve as a great incentive for you to apply for work-study on the FAFSA. Many students don't apply because they think they can earn a better salary at a nonwork-study position. This may be true—but their nonwork-study wages will hurt their financial aid eligibility.

Some students answer *no* to the question on the FAFSA that asks "In addition to grants, are you interested in work-study?" under the mistaken impression that by answering *yes* they are forfeiting grant aid or that they will be obligated to accept work-study. You can always decline work-study after it has been awarded. However, it is difficult to acquire it once classes begin.

AmeriCorps

Since 1994, more than 250,000 people nationwide have participated in AmeriCorps, a national service program with outstanding benefits, to help pay for college. AmeriCorps offers both full- and part-time positions in the fields of education, the environment, public safety, and homeland security. In addition to hourly or biweekly wages, participants can earn up to $9,450 in college assistance for two years of AmeriCorps service. This money is known as the AmeriCorps education award.

There's a hidden benefit to AmeriCorps: both the wages and the education award are exempt from calculation in the EFC. If you're just a few months away from college and have no way to pay for it without relying primarily on loans, AmeriCorps can offer one of the best short-term strategies for delaying and then paying for school. Many students have delayed college for one year or more in order to serve in AmeriCorps and have come out ahead in paying for college.

There are 10 ways AmeriCorps can help pay for college:

1. It pays members wages that are excluded from EFC calculation.
2. It offers members an education award of up to $9,450, which is excluded from EFC calculation.
3. It pays the interest accrued on current student loans for members, and these benefits are excluded from EFC calculation.
4. Anyone looking to move to a new state to gain residency should know that AmeriCorps pays travel expenses for members who relocate.
5. It offers health care and child care benefits to members.
6. AmeriCorps*VISTA offers the option of a post-service cash stipend of $1,200 for those who do not want an education award.
7. AmeriCorps*NCCC provides free room and board at its five campuses across the country.
8. It offers positions in many fields, including the environment, health and human services, public safety, and education.
9. Many of its programs have agreements with colleges that allow members to earn college credit while serving.
10. The National Service Alumni Network, at **www.nsan.org** , offers AmeriCorps alumni education and career services following program completion.

ASSETS
That Matter

The FAFSA doesn't use the term *asset*. However, it asks you to report the following five categories of assets:

1

Cash, savings, checking accounts

2

Investments, including real estate

3

Net worth of current business

4

Net worth of current farm

5

Student veteran's education benefits

The FAFSA does not consider these five items:

6

The home you live in

7

The farm on which you live and operate

8

The value of your life insurance

9

The value of your retirement plans

10

Prepaid tuition plans

Assets

An *asset* is something that has value, and the amount of assets you and your parents have affects your eligibility for financial aid.

Asset Allowance

Putting money in a child's name can be a good way for your parents to pay less in taxes—and a great way to pay *more* for college. The reason? Your parents' assets on the FAFSA have a substantial protection allowance, typically around $40,000, and any assets beyond this protection allowance are assessed at only 12 percent.

Dependent students—that's you—have no such protection and are expected to contribute 35 percent of their total assets. These assets often increase substantially around the time these students complete their first FAFSA as trust funds mature, monetary gifts from friends and family arrive, and students start putting away more money from work to pay for college costs.

Spend Your Allowance

Let's say you've just received $1,000 in graduation money and have not yet completed the FAFSA. Because cash that you have on hand is considered an asset, the federal needs analysis will assess this $1,000 at a rate of 35 percent when calculating your EFC. That results in a significant decrease in financial aid eligibility, especially since this money will probably be long gone before your first tuition bill arrives. In fact, you'll probably spend the entire amount before college even starts, on things like clothes, appliances, and supplies.

So: go shopping. Spend the money now, not later, before you complete the FAFSA. Think you'll need a dorm fridge six months from now? Get it today. Always wanted to buy a year's worth of toothpaste at the local bulk-goods

Since you have so little protection in terms of assets, you should make every effort to decrease these assets as much as possible. This could be the most appealing advice you'll ever hear: go shopping.

10
WORK-STUDY
Jobs

1

Cafeteria food server

2

Cafeteria food preparer

3

Mailroom employee

4

Housekeeper

5

Administrative assistant

6

Campus tour guide

7

Receptionist

8

Box-office ticket salesperson

9

Usher

10

Campus printing services worker

warehouse? Do it now. The less cash you have on hand when you complete your FAFSA, the more financial aid you'll receive.

Gift Postponement

Still celebrating over the advice to shop to your little heart's content? No so fast. If possible, you should do your best to *decline* gifts of money. That's right: to maximize financial aid, you should *just say no* to gifts of cash during the base income year. Otherwise, you'll wind up giving 35 percent of that money to pay for college, and you'll decrease your eligibility for aid.

If you have a grandparent or other relative who wants to give you $5,000 after high school graduation, you'd be better off asking them to hold off on that gift until your last year of college. You could also have them give the gift to your parents, whose assets are better protected under the federal needs analysis. In lieu of money, they could make purchases on your behalf. The value of a car, for example, isn't considered an asset in the federal needs analysis formula. They could even open a 529 plan for you *in their own name*. (See Chapter 2, "The Long Plan," for why this works.) Any of these options will effectively increase your financial aid eligibility by reducing your current assets.

Liabilities

Liabilities are debts. Thanks to credit cards, you and your parents might have plenty of liabilities already, before college even begins. Liabilities can also include car loans, personal loans, and loans for education.

Liabilities and Your Aid

Our society revolves around credit, and credit isn't necessarily bad. Few people would have the means to purchase homes or automobiles if they had to pay for them in cash.

Trust Funds

While trust funds do have some tax benefits, they are typically wrought with financial aid pitfalls. They are considered an asset of the student, meaning that the entire value of the trust, even if it cannot be immediately used for college costs, will be assessed at the 35 percent rate.

However, the credit card mentality has hurt many students' eligibility for financial aid. Why? Because credit card debt is not considered when calculating EFC. In other words, if you have $10,000 in your checking account but $15,000 racked up on your Visa, the federal needs-analysis formula will still assume you have $10,000 available to pay for school. Likewise, if you just bought a spiffy new Jetta and took out a hefty loan to pay for it, the loan makes no difference in the federal needs-analysis formula.

For this reason alone, you and your family should take any opportunity to *pay down consumer debt*. Look at it this way: if you have a $500 check from Grandma, you're better off putting that $500 toward your Visa balance than keeping it in the bank. If it's in the bank when you fill out the FAFSA, 35 percent of it will be considered available to pay for college. Putting that $500 toward your Visa balance makes much more sense. You'll be doing yourself a service by reducing a high-interest balance, and you'll keep that money out of reach of the financial aid calculations.

Dependency

Even though the primary responsibility of paying for college usually rests with both you *and* your parents, there may come a time when you'll need to get by on your own. When you reach this point, the Department of Education considers you independent, and they'll no longer include your parents' income and assets when calculating financial aid. This generally means you'll receive more assistance. Sound ideal? Sure it does. But becoming independent isn't easy.

Becoming Independent

The Department of Education is very clear in how it determines whether or not you can be considered independent. Seven questions appear on the FAFSA to determine whether or not this is an option for you. If you can answer *yes* to any of these questions, you won't have to supply any of your parents' financial information:

- Will you be twenty-four years old by January 1 of the current school year?
- At the beginning of the current school year, will you be working on a master's or doctorate?

- As of today, are you married?
- Do you have children who receive more than half of their support from you?
- Do you have dependents who live with you and receive more than half of their support from you, and will do so until the end of the school year?
- Are both of your parents deceased? Are you, or were you until the age of eighteen, an orphan or ward of the court?
- Are you a veteran of the U.S. Armed Forces?

Residency

If you plan to attend a public college, your state residency can substantially affect your college costs. Most public colleges charge a lower tuition for in-state residents. The difference between resident and nonresident tuition can add $50,000 or more to the cost of your education.

State Taxes

Your state residency can also impact your EFC because of a little-known allowance for state income taxes hidden deep within the federal aid rules. Though the differences are usually negligible, some students do see a change in their EFC simply by changing state residency. If, for example, your family lives in Vancouver, Washington, and decides to move five miles to the south and become residents of Portland, Oregon, your state allowance will increase by 7 percent.

What does this mean for you? If your EFC is around $3,900, this increase would suddenly make you eligible for a Pell Grant. So if you currently live in a state with no or very low state income taxes and are planning on moving to a state with a high state income tax, you might want to consider waiting to complete your FAFSA until

In terms of short-term strategies, you have very few options for being able to answer *yes* to most of these questions. However, if you were planning on getting married in the summer before college begins, it might be in your best interest to delay completing the FAFSA until after the ceremony. But remember: even though your parents' income will not be included in the needs-analysis formula, your spouse's financial information will be.

10
COMMON
Residency Requirements

1. Living within the state for at least 365 days prior to the first day of classes

2. Relinquishing residency in prior home state

3. Demonstration of financial independence

4. Unclaimed by anyone else on federal tax returns as a dependent for previous two years

5. Has not taken classes within the preceding year while attempting to gain state residency

6. Evidence of intent to establish residency, as shown by state driver's license, rental receipts dating back at least one year, employment pay stubs, etc.

7. Not receiving any health or auto insurance benefits from a parent or guardian who is not a current state resident

8. Exceptions made to military and dependents who are serving within the state where residency is sought

9. Filing of state taxes as a resident in year preceding residency request

10. Is a dependent of somebody who meets the above requirements

your residency is established. Just don't wait beyond your school's priority deadline.

Residency Requirements

Residency requirements vary greatly from state to state and are often very strict. If your heart is set on attending a public college in another state, you need to find out the residency requirements as soon as possible. Many students are able to gain state residency by moving to and working in a state for at least one year.

Taking Extra Time

Some strategies for paying for college, such as state residency or gaining independent status, might be within your reach if you had a little more time to work with. Some students decide to maximize their options by giving themselves that time. *Stop outs* are students who either leave college or delay enrollment but fully intend to begin or return and graduate. The reasons to become a stop out are not exclusively related to financial aid, of course, but the benefits regarding financial aid are significant.

Family Matters

As we mentioned in Chapter 2, "The Long Plan," the number of siblings attending college at the same time as you has a significant impact on your EFC. If your younger brother or sister is only a year behind you, stopping out—delaying college—for one year will cut both your EFCs in half.

By the same token, if you expect to have a child, or your parents expect to have another child, you might benefit from delaying enrollment until those new family members have arrived. The FAFSA is very clear that these new family members must arrive by July 1 of the current school year and continue to receive more than half of their support from either you or your parents until June 30 of the following year.

The exception to this rule concerns unborn children. The FAFSA actually says that if you or your parents are expecting a child to be born before July 1 of the end of your first year of college, then you may include them now as family members. In fact, if your doctor has informed you that you are expecting multiple births, you may count each child as a current dependent. However, even though the FAFSA allows unborn children to count toward family size, it does not allow unborn children to influence dependency status. Even exceptions to the rule have their own exceptions when it comes to financial aid.

In determining parental contributions toward dependent student costs, the federal needs analysis allows for a little more flexibility than institutional needs analysis. For the FAFSA, students must report the income and assets of the parent they live with the most and his or her spouse, if any. When parents are divorced, this can get complicated.

Residency

Since gaining state residency is usually such a strict process, you may find yourself faced with delaying enrollment for up to one year. Unfortunately, many students enroll in public colleges as nonresidents, thinking that they might qualify for in-state tuition in subsequent years. However, most colleges make this a difficult prospect: residency is rarely granted to students who are full-time students and have applied for residency only to take advantage of in-state tuition rates. They're wise to your sneaky ways. Surprised? Sometimes, waiting an extra year is all you can do to give yourself the best chance of establishing residency.

Age

Many students who are in their early twenties might have additional incentive to postpone college enrollment, since independent status is granted to those who are twenty-four years old before January 1 of the current school year. Even if you don't turn twenty-four by your first year of college, postponing enrollment might help you gain independent status and potentially receive more financial aid for your sophomore, junior, and/or senior year of college.

Panic Plan

Despite all your planning, saving, and applying, there's a chance you might still be unable to pay for college. In addition, you might not be willing to postpone your education. Things might seem desperate, but here's an unexpected ray of light: the community and technical college system.

The Community College System

It might not seem very glamorous. You might think you're too "good" for it. You've always risen above expectations, and your goals are high, indeed. However, many students in your same situation have discovered the hidden benefits of being a big fish in a little pond. Small class sizes, full transfer agreements to the big four-year schools, teachers with Ph.D.s who don't make you refer to them as "Doctor" . . . Not convinced? How about this: *tuition is often half the cost of even public universities.*

More Bang for Your Buck

Many bright students consider community college as a short-term strategy for paying for college. For students with few other options, this can be an excellent method of saving a considerable amount of money before transferring to a four-year school.

Students' and Professors' Choice

Community and technical colleges draw good students, but they are also drawing more and more professors who want to spend their time in the classroom actually teaching, as opposed to those in the publish-or-perish research environment of the modern university system.

QUIRKY FAFSA
Divorce Regulations

1   Custodial refers to the parent with whom the student lived the most in the previous year, even if this parent provided less financial support than the noncustodial parent.

2   The custodial parent is not necessarily the same as the parent who has legal custody.

3   The custodial parent is not necessarily the same as the parent who claimed the child on his or her tax returns.

4   If the dependent student did not live with either parent, then the custodial parent is the one who provided the most support over the previous twelve months.

5   If neither parent provided any support, then the custodial parent is the one who provided the most support for the most recent calendar year in which support was provided.

6   Any child support or alimony from the noncustodial parent must still be reported on the FAFSA.

7   If the custodial parent remarries, then the stepparent must provide financial information on the dependent student's FAFSA, even if the marriage was not in existence in the previous year and even if the dependent student has never lived with or met the stepparent.

8   Prenuptial agreements have no impact on the FAFSA, and stepparents must provide financial information, even if the prenuptial agreement absolves the new spouse from funding the stepchild's education.

9   The Hope and Lifetime Learning Tax Credits may be taken only by the parent who claims the student as a dependent for federal tax purposes, even if that parent is the noncustodial parent for financial aid reasons. This means that the educational tax credit can be taken by a parent who did not pay for the tuition for which he or she is receiving credit.

10 A noncustodial parent who provides more than half of the student's support does not need to report his or her financial information on the student's FAFSA. But he or she may still include that noncustodial child as part of family size for any other children completing the FAFSA, and for whom he or she is the custodial parent. This means that this parent can use the child to his or her own advantage—without ever having to give any help to that child in return.

4

THE FREE MONEY

"Sandy said, 'When I grow up I'm going to be a banker and make money. Someone in this family has to stay in the real world.'"

Madeleine L'Engle
A Wind in the Door

Free money consists of much more than just grants and scholarships. Knowing all the options may give you an edge in your ultimate goal: getting someone *else* to pay for *your* education.

The Meaning of *Free*

The financial aid counselors you meet probably won't use the term *free money*—it's hard to convince a financial aid counselor that anything is truly free. If you eavesdrop on a financial aid meeting, you'll probably hear them talk about *gift aid* and *self-help aid*. *Gift aid* is money given to you that you don't have to repay, such as a grant or scholarship. *Self-help aid* is money you either have to repay or earn beforehand, such as loans or college work-study.

The Ratio

Each financial aid office has the right to set a ratio of gift aid to self-help aid that meets its overall funding and enrollment goals. After the financial aid officers determine your need, they will use this ratio to decide how much of your need will be met by scholarships and how much will be met by less favorable aid, such as loans.

You should request this ratio from the colleges you're applying to. Different schools handle the ratio different ways, and their methods can make a difference in your aid package. For example, some schools actually reward students for bringing in private scholarships by including these as self-help aid. You did *earn* that scholarship through hard work, right? Other schools will simply award you more loans, rather than institutional scholarships, to meet your remaining need.

The Pell Grant

The Pell Grant, by the Department of Education's account, is the foundation upon which the neediest students can build their dreams of a higher education. In terms of a dollar amount, the main source of free money available for college is the U.S. government, and the largest of the free federal programs is the Pell Grant. For 2004, the amount of individual Pell Grants range from $400 up to $4,050.

Eligibility

In order to receive a Pell Grant, you must be a U.S. citizen or eligible noncitizen who has not yet earned a bachelor's or graduate degree. You are eligible to receive only one Pell Grant per year and cannot receive Pell Grant funds from more than one school at a time.

How to Apply

The FAFSA serves as the application for the Pell Grant. You will also need to complete any financial aid applications for your specific school, though they will not affect the amount of your grant. The Department of Education creates a list of tables each year that specifies the Pell Grant amount a student can receive based on numerous factors, including the student's EFC, COA, and enrollment status (full-time, half-time, or less than half-time).

> "I had a student who started school in the spring semester and didn't complete the FAFSA because he thought all the financial aid would be gone. I convinced him otherwise, and he wound up with a $2,000 Pell Grant. Some financial aid programs are always there if you qualify."
>
> **Brian**
> **Financial Aid**
> **Administrator**

Pell Grant Secrets

The Pell Grant is the best kind of free money—you never have to repay it, and you don't have to do anything to earn it except fill out the FAFSA. You might think that since the Pell Grant is tied directly to your EFC, you can't do anything to increase the amount of your award. However, there are three secrets you should know to maximize your chances of getting a Pell—and getting the largest Pell possible.

> In 2004, the Pell Grant program had a budget of $12.7 billion.

Secret #1: Cost of Attendance

The amount of Pell Grant you receive is directly tied not only to your EFC but also to your COA. If you increase your COA, you could wind up with a larger grant.

For example, the Department of Education offers Pell Grants to students with EFCs between $3,801 and $3,850 *only if* their COA is at least $4,000. So if your EFC is $3,850 and your COA is $3,999, then you will receive no Pell

10
KINDS OF
Free Money

1

Federal Grants

2

State Grants

3

Private Scholarships

4

Institutional Scholarships

5

Federal Scholarships

6

Service Rewards

7

Fellowships

8

Housing Allowances

9

Tuition Waivers

10

Forgivable Loans

Grant. However, if you increase your COA by just one dollar to $4,000, suddenly you're receiving a $400 Pell Grant. You can see how the Pell Grant amounts are calculated by checking out the Pell Grant tables. (See sidebar for more information.)

Increasing your COA might be as simple as writing a letter to the financial aid administrator explaining that you have additional school-related expenses coming up, such as the purchase of a computer.

Secret #2: Course Load

The Pell Grant is also tied to the number of classes you take and whether you're a part-time or a full-time student. Sometimes, by taking just one more class, you can gain a Pell Grant. For example, if your college requires you to take four classes to be considered a full-time student and you're taking only three, you won't be eligible for a Pell even if your EFC is $3,801 and your cost of attendance is $15,000. If you enroll in just one more class, voila—you're now receiving a $400 Pell Grant, primarily because you've changed from part-time to full-time status.

If you attend a public university or community college, you might even *profit* from taking just one more credit hour. However, even if that additional class costs you more than $400, you're still going to need a certain amount of credits to graduate. You might as well have the Pell Grant program pay for as many of those credits as possible.

Remember: the lower your EFC, the greater the potential increase in Pell Grant amount. Let's say you have an EFC of $1,000 and a COA of $1,299 and are enrolled in only two classes, which makes you a half-time student. If you take two additional classes, raising your COA to $4,000, you can wind up with more than $3,000 in Pell Grant aid.

Secret #3: Deadlines

Your eligibility for the Pell Grant and the amount of the Pell Grant you receive are tied to three things: your EFC, your COA, and your status as a part-time or full-time student.

Surprise, surprise—*the Pell Grant has no deadline.* The Pell Grant is known as an entitlement program. Unlike the vast majority of other grant and scholarship programs, the Pell Grant does not run out. If you are eligible to receive a Pell Grant, you *will* receive one, even if your college says they're out of other aid.

You can receive a Pell Grant even if you apply after classes have already begun. In fact, if you have been attending college all year and for whatever reason never completed the FAFSA, you can still receive Pell Grant money—even for prior academic quarters. This is known as *retroactive payment.* Even if you don't apply for financial aid until the summer quarter following your first year in college, you can still receive all the Pell Grant money to which you were entitled during the previous year. Now *that's* called getting what you deserve.

The SEOG

To maximize your chances of getting a SEOG, submit the FAFSA as soon as you possibly can.

Besides the Pell Grant, the other major federal grant program is the Supplemental Educational Opportunity Grant (SEOG). The maximum amount of this grant is similar to the Pell Grant, weighing in at $4,000 per year.

Eligibility

Unlike the Pell Grant, the SEOG is not an entitlement. The SEOG is known as a *campus-based program,* which means that just because you qualify for a SEOG doesn't mean you'll get one. Campus-based programs are limited, and the criteria for receiving them depend on each campus's own guidelines. Some students who are not eligible to receive a Pell Grant might still receive a full SEOG. However, when awarding SEOGs, most college financial aid offices give the greatest priority to students who have the lowest EFCs.

The SEOG Secret

Want a SEOG? Apply as soon as you possibly can. *That's* the SEOG secret. Most colleges run out of SEOG money when they package their first batch of applications, so if you wait until March or April to complete the FAFSA, you've likely already missed the boat.

Keep in mind: turning in your FAFSA early maximizes your chances of getting a SEOG, but it doesn't *guarantee* you'll get one. Since each financial aid office sets its own guidelines for awarding SEOGs, you should contact the schools where you are applying to find out how these grants are awarded and what the qualifications are.

State Grants

Uncle Sam isn't the only one concerned about your education. Each state plus the District of Columbia has a higher education agency that oversees financial aid programs specific to state residents. Most of these states offer some pretty enticing reasons for staying close to home and attending either a public or private college in your state of residency. In fact, some states offer grants that can exceed $10,000 per year!

In Chapter 6, "The State System," we'll give you the strategies you need to make the most of state offerings, including grants and scholarships.

Scholarships

You can win scholarships for any number of accomplishments, including athletics, academics, and music. There are scholarships available for students of certain ethnic backgrounds and scholarships for outstanding essays. In other words, there's most likely a scholarship for you that will be a perfect fit. In case you forgot . . . scholarships are *free money.* You need to know how to find—and get—a scholarship to help pay for college. You also need to know how scholarships affect your overall aid package.

Private Scholarships

Private scholarships, or outside scholarships, can come from anyone and anywhere for any number of reasons. These are generally scholarships you pursue on your own, independent of the colleges to which you apply.

Federal scholarships seem to be the least publicized and least well-known financial aid awards in existence—even some financial aid officers are unaware of them. An easy place to start your search for federal scholarships is the Department of Education website at **www.ed.gov.** Simply type *scholarship* into the search box.

Scholarships are always good, right? Not so fast. Most colleges count private scholarships as gift aid when calculating your financial aid award. This means that if you receive a scholarship, you may end up with more loans to cover your remaining need and fewer institutional scholarships, grants, or work-study. If your COA is $20,000 and you win a scholarship for $15,000, that means you can now receive only an additional $5,000 worth of financial aid.

How the financial aid office treats that remaining $5,000 of need may make all the difference in the world, and this is a very good example of why you should apply to more than one college. By comparing different award letters, you'll be able to see which colleges will use that private scholarship in a way that leaves you with the least amount of graduation debt.

Institutional Scholarships

Institutional scholarships typically come from the college's endowment or foundation, and financial aid offices will almost certainly consider them as gift aid. Though you should still apply for all the institutional scholarships you can, you might want to ask the financial aid office how these scholarships will impact your other financial aid. Each year, countless students are dismayed to find out that their financial aid award letters are adjusted with higher loan amounts after they win institutional scholarships. The financial aid officer will probably give you that look that says, "Stop complaining—you got a scholarship, after all." But if you've received a similar award offer from another college with a higher gift aid to self-help ratio, you can return that look with a choice one of your own.

Federal Scholarships

In addition to private and institutional scholarships, there are also several federally funded scholarship programs out there. The Byrd Scholarship (www.ed.gov/programs/iduesbyrd), with average awards of $1,500, is offered in all fifty states, usually based on academic or extracurricular merit. Application information is available through each state's higher education board or through your high school guidance counselor. Truman Scholarships (www.truman.gov) provide $26,000 to seventy to eighty undergraduate students each year based on leadership and public service skills. Truman Scholars are nominated by the college, so it's a good excuse to practice those networking skills as soon as you've gotten your bearings on campus.

Remember: these are free! Paying for access to a scholarship search service is usually a waste of your money.

Reporting Scholarships

You are required to report any scholarships you receive to the financial aid office since they count as resources. As with most financial aid tasks, the sooner you do this, the better. Many students make the mistake of waiting until the last minute to report this money, thinking that once a financial aid office has sent out an award letter it will not reduce the amount of grants or institutional scholarships. You are likely to find, however, that financial aid offices can and often do reduce the amount of institutional gift aid when they discover a student has unreported scholarship dollars.

The best advice is to report your scholarships as soon as you know you'll receive them. You should find out beforehand what effect outside scholarships will have on your overall financial aid. That way, you can compare the different financial aid packages and choose where to spend your tuition dollars based on the best offer. If you wait until after you've committed to attending a college, you'll lose that additional leverage.

Scholarships and the Pell Grant

To maximize your financial aid, *submit the FAFSA even if you've gotten a lot of outside scholarship money.* If you're eligible for a Pell Grant, you can still receive that Pell Grant even if you win a full scholarship. The Pell Grant is an entitlement

10
SCHOLARSHIP
Essay Tips

1. Ask the college how the applications are rated and if there is a scoring scale you can see.

2. Ask if you can look at past successful essays.

3. Request a list of current or past award winners. Those students might be willing to give you hints or advice on what worked.

4. Read the instructions very carefully and address any qualifications directly and often.

5. Rather than list your attributes, tell a story that illustrates them.

6. Don't be afraid to take a chance. Show your humorous or creative side.

7. Meet as many different staff members as you can, being as nice as possible and identifying yourself by name. When a scholarship reviewer can associate a face with an application, it makes it that much harder to say no.

8. Before you begin writing, delete the Comic Sans font from your computer. Your letter should look clean and professional.

9. Under no circumstances submit an essay with any spelling or grammatical errors.

10. Follow up with a thank-you note, even if you don't get the award. The saying "There's always next time" doesn't apply to anyone who whines and complains to the scholarship committee.

program, which means you'll receive the amount of Pell Grant for which you are eligible, even if all your other scholarships equal your COA. This is one of the few cases in which you can receive financial aid in excess of your COA.

10 Scholarship Contests

Is there anything more American than a contest? Even if you've been lax in your studies or lazy on your SATs, a contest offers you the chance to roll the dice and make the world right again in one fell swoop. Unfortunately, as your instincts are almost assuredly telling you, many contests are likely to be set-ups, with the only real winners being those smart enough not to play. You should be skeptical of any scholarship contest application you receive, particularly if there are any fees involved.

For those of you who simply cannot control your urge to compete, here is a list of ten legitimate, and free, scholarship contests.

1. Think you have a great idea for making the world a kinder place? Try entering the National Peace Essay Contest (**www.usip.org**).

2. Or maybe you don't see what's so great about peace, love, and under-standing. In that case, maybe the Principles of War Essay Contest (**www.usni.org**) is the way to go.

3. Maybe you just want to make the world a greener place. Voila: the Better Earth Environmental Essay Contest awaits (**www.abetterearth.org**).

4. Did you save all those A+ Civics papers? The National Endowment for the Humanities is dying to hear your "Idea of America" (**www.wethepeople.gov**).

5. Even better, the Society for Professional Journalists (**www.spj.org**) wants to know "What does a free media mean to America?" So send in your essay.

6. You can enter the Free Will and Personal Responsibility Essay Contest (**www.intothebest.com**), especially since you've surely stayed up countless nights asking yourself, "Would I rather be liked or respected?"

7. Speaking of tough questions: is your favorite president Abraham Lincoln? (**www.thelincolnforum.org**)

8. . . . or John F. Kennedy? (**www.jfkcontest.org**)

10

FREE
Scholarship Search Engines

Most of these search engines will ask you to register a user name and password. Although they are free, you should note that in exchange for this service many of these websites will ask for your contact information and/or require you to look at advertisements. You should never give out any financial or personal records, such as your social security number or checking/savings account information.

1
www.fastweb.com

2
www.studentaid.ed.gov

3
www.srnexpress.com

4
www.collegenet.com

5
www.wiredscholar.com

6
www.gocollege.com

7
www.fastaid.com

8
www.collegeview.com

9
www.collegeboard.com

10
www.scholarships.com

9. Are you the one kid in class who really gets Ayn Rand? There's a scholarship contest out there for you too. (**www.aynrand.org**).

10. Maybe, just maybe, the only thing you really understand is good old-fashioned Duck Tape. It's good to know that **www.ducktapeclub.com** exists.

The Scholarship Essay

If you're applying for a scholarship, you'll almost always have to write an essay. Who will read your scholarship essay? You'll spend hours—or days—writing it, so you should know who ultimately reviews it. At many schools, volunteers are recruited to read the dozens or hundreds of essays for the few scholarships available. These volunteers are generally college staff, alumni, and sometimes even current students. They receive score cards, a stack of random scholarship essays, a pat on the back, and, usually, a very short deadline.

You might hope your essay will be read carefully and thoroughly by a person in a business suit with a degree in dialectics during the middle of the day in a quiet, well-lit conference room. However, the reality is probably quite different. Your essay is likely being quickly scanned by an underpaid or unpaid staff member on a Thursday night between bites of pizza during TV commercial breaks.

When writing your essay, you might want to think about this person. Does your essay merely list your qualifications, or does it tell a story that even the most distracted, absent-minded reader is likely to remember?

Scholarship Scams

Many students seeking scholarships fall victim each year to scholarship fraud. Don't be one of them! You should be wary of any solicitations that promise you scholarships or low-interest loans, even though they might sound like incredible deals. Most scholarship scams involve ask-

"My family paid $800 for a 'guaranteed' scholarship service. In the end, I didn't get any scholarships, and I couldn't get a refund of my $800 because I couldn't prove that I applied for every scholarship they sent me. But I didn't even qualify for most of them!"

Martin, 19

ing you to pay up-front fees, "guaranteeing" that you'll receive money for college. Legitimate scholarship search websites will never require you to pay a fee for their services, and, unfortunately, there is never any guarantee that you will win the scholarship you want.

Scholarship scams are such a problem that the Federal Trade Commission conducted an investigation into the countless complaints of scholarship fraud nationwide and released a report that detailed how eight such companies were able to swindle 175,000 students out of $22 million. Don't be a victim!

Service Awards

You can earn free money for school simply by giving a little of yourself and your time. Service work looks great on a resume too.

AmeriCorps

As we mentioned in Chapter 2, "The Long Plan," AmeriCorps offers up to nearly $10,000 in scholarships for those who perform community service. If you use the AmeriCorps education award to repay student loans, you don't have to report it to the financial aid office, which means it won't reduce your other financial aid. Visit **www.americorps.org** for all the details.

The Armed Forces

Service in one of the armed forces is a popular choice for students looking for a lot of free money for college. The amounts can seem quite high, and advertisements often claim that you'll receive up to $50,000 for college. If you explore this option, be sure to find out exactly how much you'll actually receive. The amount will vary considerably based on which type of military service you choose, how long you sign up for, how long you attend college, and what kind of degree you decide to pursue.

If you decide that military service is the right choice for you, find out as soon as possible if the college you want to attend has a financial aid officer who specializes in Veteran's Administration (VA) benefits. This person will be a vital resource, especially since the impact of VA benefits on your other financial aid can be extremely complicated.

Fellowships

A fellowship is free money generally in the form of a stipend that is awarded for a specific project, purpose, or skill, but it can also be awarded based on need. The word *fellowship* typically conjures up images of bookish graduate students walking a thin line between breakthrough research and severe sleep deprivation. Though most fellowships are indeed awarded to graduate students, many fellowships are available for undergrads as well. In recent years, many community foundations have changed their former scholarship programs into fellowships.

You are unlikely to find fellowships by searching through the typical scholarship books or websites. More and more, fellowships are offered by community-based nonprofit groups who see the value of combining their philanthropic giving with educational opportunities.

How They Work

Fellowships are a type of financial aid that you don't have to repay. Like scholarships, some fellowships are paid directly to the school for tuition, fees, and education-related expenses. In these instances, they count as a financial resource, usually as gift aid. If you receive one of these kinds of fellowships, you need to report it to the financial aid office, and they will probably adjust your other aid. Some fellowships, however, are really more similar to jobs, and in fact do not require concurrent college enrollment. An example would be the White House Fellows program (**www.whitehouse.gov/fellows**), which each year, for around ten individuals with exceptional public service and leadership skills, provides the opportunity to work as full-time paid special assistants to senior White House staff.

Other kinds of fellowships are really more similar to rewards for past work or service. The Tacoma, Washington-based Jane's Fellowship (www. trff.org), offered by the Russell Family Foundation, is an example. This fellowship pays six to ten individuals a $10,000 stipend to implement community-strengthening projects of their choice. Many communities have foundations that offer this kind of opportunity to those enterprising enough to seek them out.

Hidden Free Money

By now you're an old pro at searching for scholarships and grants through Google or Yahoo, and you've also scoured the scholarship engines at websites like FastWeb. There are two additional sources of free money to keep in mind.

Tuition Waivers

Have you ever done a search for the phrase *tuition waiver*? Try it—and you'll discover a whole new world of financial aid opportunities. Tuition waivers are basically the college telling you not to worry about some of the tuition, and colleges offer them for several reasons. Colleges struggling to recruit more students might use tuition waivers as a way to attract particular students who might not have the credentials needed to win an institutional scholarship. Some schools offer waivers for students who are children of college employees. Still other schools offer waivers to students who work for the college, especially graduate students who serve as teaching assistants.

Housing Allowances

Some schools offer substantial discounts in the form of housing allowances to students who serve as resident assistants in the college dorm. You'll get to live on campus for free in exchange for your service, which might include organizing dorm activities, serving as a link to the student counseling service, or being a mediator for roommate conflicts. You'll generally apply for a resident assistant position after you begin school.

How They Work

Unlike scholarships, tuition waivers are typically not well publicized, and the reason is that scholarships and tuition waivers usually come from two different sources. Whereas scholarships are funded through endowments, which means they are usually available year after year for approximately the same amount, tuition waivers are more often taken out of college operating budgets. Because operating budgets are highly variable from year to year, tuition waivers are less publicized.

As with outside scholarships, you should ask the financial aid office if tuition waivers and housing allowances are treated as self-help or gift aid. Since a waiver may come as an exchange for work, such as with resident assistant housing allowances, you'll want to make the case that this is self-help aid and that the financial aid office shouldn't reduce your other gift aid.

Loan Forgiveness

You don't need forgiveness for having a loan . . . but if your loan is forgiven, you won't have to pay it back.

Depending on what you'd like to study and where you attend college, you might have access to student loans that have some remarkable benefits. Many states, for example, offer student loans to future teachers that have partial or full forgiveness provisions. In other words, these are loans you may not have to pay back if you fulfill certain requirements.

What makes these loans free money is how financial aid offices view them. Unlike scholarships or grants, forgivable loans are virtually always considered self-help programs. Even though they act very much in the same way as the other types of free money, they're often better since they won't reduce your other gift aid.

If you graduate and decide you no longer want to agree to the forgiveness provisions of the loan, you'll have to repay these loans in full and often at higher rates than those for Stafford or Perkins loans. Before signing up, make sure you have a clear idea of both the benefits and the consequences of these programs. We'll discuss these programs in more detail in Chapter 5, "The Loans."

Taxation

What Uncle Sam giveth, he sometimes partially taketh away. For the most part, you have very little to worry about. Pell Grants, scholarships, and tuition waivers are protected from taxation under IRS exceptions, as long as they're used for tuition and school-related expenses. However, if you receive any awards that offer money beyond the COA or include additional money for nonrelated expenses, you should consult with your accountant to find out what you need to report to the financial aid office. The penalties for not doing so might negate all that hard work it took to get the money in the first place.

Good and True

Does all this free money sound too good to be true? Don't worry—free money is really out there. This might be your first (only?) smile elicited by financial aid information. Free money is the best you can get. A little hard work, some sleuthing, and a wise wariness of scams go a long way toward big payoffs.

5 THE LOANS

"Every year we get complaints from students who used 'alternative' loans. If you have to borrow for college, your best bet is to take advantage of one of the federal student loan programs."

Tom
Financial Aid Administrator

Around thirty years ago, the idea of borrowing through a student loan program to pay for college seemed extreme. In 1974, a full Pell Grant covered almost 85 percent of the tuition at an average four-year public university. In 2002, however, the federal government issued more than 11 million loans worth more than $40 billion, compared to less than $8 billion in Pell Grants.

For most students, borrowing is a matter of when, not if.

10 Loan Basics

How you borrow is just as important as *how much* you borrow. Different borrowing programs have different interest rates, repayment plans, and loan limits, and the choices you make now will affect you for the next ten years—the average time it takes to repay a student loan. In order to choose the loan program that's right for you, you need to understand ten basic things about loans.

1. Need-based loans

Loans based on need, such as the Perkins loan or the subsidized Stafford loan, are usually the best borrowing options, with low interest rates and generous repayment options. Some financial aid offices may choose to use these student loans instead of institutional scholarships or grants in order to meet your overall need.

2. Nonneed-based loans

Loans not based on need generally have higher interest rates and stricter repayment options than need-based loans.

3. Subsidized loans

Subsidized means that while you are enrolled in school at least half-time, the federal government will pay any interest that accrues on your loans.

4. Unsubsidized loans

With unsubsidized loans, you are responsible for any accrued interest as soon as the loan is issued.

5. Deferment

Deferment allows you to postpone loan repayment as long as you are enrolled in school at least half-time. Deferment applies mainly to federal student loans. During deferment of subsidized Stafford loans and Perkins loans, the federal government will pay any interest that accrues. You are responsible for repaying the interest on any unsubsidized loans during deferment.

6. Forbearance

A lender will grant you forbearance when you are unable to make your loan payments because of financial hardship, unusual circumstances, or participation in a national service program such as AmeriCorps. Forbearance is a temporary reprieve, not a permanent solution, and the federal government does not pay the interest the loan accrues during this time. You'll have to pay up eventually.

7. Grace period

A loan's grace period is the period of time before you have to begin repaying your loan. A grace period usually begins as soon as you graduate from college or drop below half-time enrollment. Stafford loans have a six-month grace period, while Perkins loans offer a grace period of nine months.

8. Origination fees

You pay origination fees in order to receive a loan. Origination fees are used to cover the administrative costs of student loans and vary greatly depending on the type of loan. Perkins loans have no origination fees, while private student loans have origination fees that can exceed 10 percent.

9. Guarantee fees

Guarantee fees are essentially insurance coverage for students who don't pay back their loans. These fees can vary greatly from loan to loan, but they are lowest with the federal student loans and highest among the nonguaranteed private student loans.

10. Default

If you fail to pay your student loan, you are in default. Defaulting on a student loan will prevent you from receiving any future financial aid until you pay up. There's no easy way out: you can't get rid of a defaulted student

LOAN
Programs

1
Perkins loan

2
Subsidized Stafford loan

3
Unsubsidized Stafford loan

4
PLUS loan

5
Alternative (or Private) loans

6
Consolidation loans

7
Emergency loans

8
Forgivable loans

9
Home equity loans

10
State loan programs

loan by declaring bankruptcy. Defaulting on a loan can severely impact your credit rating and can lead to garnishment of your wages and/or withholdings from any federal income tax refunds. In other words, you won't get your paycheck or tax return—your lender will. And finally, one more reason not to go into default (as if you needed one): you can't get either deferment or forbearance on a defaulted loan.

Each year, approximately 6 percent of students default on their loans. Should you add your name to that list, you can expect the following:

- Garnishment of your wages, up to 10 percent of your take-home pay
- Withholding of tax refunds ("tax offset")
- A drop in your credit rating that could prevent you from receiving auto or home loans
- Endless phone calls and letters from the collection agency hired to recover your past-due loan
- Full responsibility for any legal/recovery fees generated in the attempt to collect on your loan balance
- Ineligibility for any deferments on your other federal loans
- Potential lawsuits to recover the loan amount you owe
- Ineligibility for any other financial aid
- Ineligibility for loan forgiveness or repayment programs
- That unpleasant feeling that comes with irresponsibility

The Perkins Loan

Established in 1958 under the National Defense Student Loan Program, the federal Perkins loan is one of the oldest forms of financial aid—and one of the best loans available.

What Gives?

The government funds the Perkins loan, but colleges administer it, which means the college is the lender. When you begin repayment, you'll send your money back to the college. If you have any questions about your loan, you'll need to talk directly with your school. Some students see this as a benefit.

WAYS TO
Discharge Your Perkins Loan

The Perkins loan offers several ways to fully or partially discharge the amount you owe. See your school for details about any of the following circumstances:

1 Disability after receiving the Perkins loan

2 Employment in Head Start

3 Employment in law enforcement/corrections

4 Employment as a nurse/medical technician

5 Employment as a professional provider of early intervention services for the disabled

6 Employment in a public/nonprofit child or family service agency

7 Employment as a teacher

8 Employment in the armed forces

9 Participation in VISTA or the Peace Corps

10 School closure prior to completion of your degree

Who Gets?

Not every college participates in the Perkins loan program, and even colleges that do participate usually have a very limited amount of money to distribute. If you want a Perkins loan, you should complete the FAFSA and institutional financial aid applications *as soon as possible.*

Perkins Pros

The Perkins loan is as good as it gets when it comes to borrowing. The interest rate is set at 5 percent, repayment does not begin until nine months after you graduate or drop below half-time status, and there are no origination or guarantee fees. Students can typically borrow up to $20,000 for undergraduate studies, $4,000 per year. The Perkins loan can also be forgiven or discharged in a number of ways.

Perkins Cons

Although many students view the Perkins loan as the best loan, you should be aware of its drawbacks. First, recently the interest rates of subsidized Stafford loans have been lower than the fixed 5 percent rate of the Perkins loan, which means that, for now, subsidized Stafford loans are actually the better option. Though these low rates will probably not last, this is still a good reason to ask about current Stafford loan rates before blindly accepting the Perkins loan.

Another drawback concerns loan consolidation, where you combine your loans and make just one monthly payment. As you'll see in a moment, federal loan consolidation can be a great way of repaying multiple loans, but if the only loan you have is a Perkins loan, you can't consolidate it.

The Stafford Loan

Originally known as the Guaranteed Student Loan, the Stafford loan is now the largest single financial aid program in existence, with more than $25 billion borrowed in 2002. When students or financial aid administrators talk about student loans, they are almost always referring to the Stafford program.

In order to borrow a Stafford loan, you must complete the FAFSA Stafford loans are far more abundant than the Perkins loan or Supplemental

Educational Opportunity Grant, so completing your FAFSA late will probably not affect your Stafford eligibility.

Subsidized Versus Unsubsidized

There are two kinds of Stafford loans: subsidized and unsubsidized. The main difference between them is who pays the interest and when. The federal government will pay any interest on subsidized Stafford loans while you are enrolled in college at least half-time. Since students typically take five or more years to graduate, this benefit can be substantial. Subsidized Stafford loans are given based on need.

The government does not pay the interest on your unsubsidized Stafford loan at any time, which makes it a less favorable form of aid than the subsidized Stafford. As soon as you get the loan, interest will begin to accrue. However, you can choose to defer payment of this interest in a process known as capitalization. This means that the interest is added to the principal of the loan upon graduation, and you can pay it all off together. You can qualify for the unsubsidized Stafford loan regardless of need.

Interest

The interest rate of the Stafford loan is capped at 8.25 percent. However, it can fall substantially lower than this, since it's a variable-rate loan (which means it follows the rate set by the Federal Reserve). In fact, it hit an all-time low of 3.37 percent in July 2004. Also important to understand is that the interest rate of the Stafford loan is actually 0.6 percent lower while you are in school and during your grace period.

Maximum Loan Amounts

If you are a dependent student, the maximum amount of Stafford loan you can borrow each year, whether subsidized or unsubsidized, depends on how far along you are in school:

- Freshmen: up to $2,625
- Sophomores: up to $3,500
- Juniors and seniors: up to $5,500
- Graduate students: up to $8,500

The amount of Stafford loan that is subsidized depends on how much financial need exists. For example, if your EFC is $0, then the entire amount of your regular Stafford loan will be subsidized because your need is greater. If your EFC is greater than your COA, however, the entire amount of your regular Stafford loan will be unsubsidized.

Additional Stafford Loans

Independent students, as well as dependent students whose families are turned down for a PLUS loan, may borrow an additional amount of Stafford loan beyond the maximum amounts listed above. This additional Stafford loan is always unsubsidized, and the amount you can borrow each year depends on your year in school:

- Freshmen and sophomores: up to $4,000
- Juniors and seniors: up to $5,000
- Graduate students: up to $10,000

The total lifetime amounts that students can borrow through the Stafford program are considerable:

- Dependent students may borrow a total of up to $23,000 for their undergraduate education.
- Independent students, as well as dependent students turned down for PLUS loans, may borrow up to $46,000 for their undergraduate education, no more than $23,000 of which can be subsidized.
- Graduate students, when combining their limits with the total undergraduate limit, can borrow up to a whopping $138,500.

Fees

Stafford loans, unlike Perkins loans, also come with origination and guarantee fees. These fees cover the administrative costs needed to run the Stafford program, as well as provide insurance against those students who default

If you have a high amount of unsubsidized Stafford loan, you might be able to increase the amount of subsidized Stafford loan by increasing your COA. You can do this legitimately by documenting any unusual expenses, such as medical care, child care, or school equipment costs.

on their loans. The fees are usually up to 1 percent for guarantee and up to 3 percent for origination. However, many lenders are now offering more competitive guarantee and/or origination fees. If you are borrowing a Stafford loan at a school that allows you to use private lenders, make sure that you shop around for the best deals.

Lenders

Check It Yourself

The Department of Education allows anyone with a Perkins or Stafford loan to check their loan amount online at the National Student Loan Data System. Visit **www. nslds.ed.gov** to sign up.

If your school participates in the Federal Direct Student Loan program, then the school is your lender. If your school participates in the Federal Family Educational Loan Program, as most schools do, then you may select a lender of your choosing. These schools will often have a list of preferred lenders and will encourage you to use one of them rather than a lender who is not on the list. The advantage to using a preferred lender is that they typically have close relationships with the financial aid office, even allowing the school to access their computer databases. This often translates into quicker loan-processing times.

Don't let this dissuade you from using a lender of your choosing who is not on the preferred lenders list. For example, your credit union may also process Stafford loans and might give you financial benefits, such as no origination fees or lower interest rates, if you go with them. Just be sure to let the financial aid office know your intentions early on. This should help you avoid any delays in processing.

Paying It Back

No more than 10 percent of your gross monthly income should be devoted to paying off student loans.

Student loans often represent the first time a person borrows money, and because of this, students don't always have a full grasp of how difficult it can be to pay the money back. Here's an example: if you borrow the lifetime maximum of $138,500 for your undergraduate and graduate education, you're on a ten-year repayment schedule, and the interest rate is the maximum 8.5 percent, *your monthly loan payment will be almost $1,700!* Loan officers recommend that no more than 10 percent of your gross monthly income should be devoted to paying off your student loans, so, in this case, your annual salary would need to be at least $200,000 in order to comfortably repay your student debt.

You may be reluctant to decline the Stafford loans listed on your financial aid award letter. However, you should be careful not to borrow more than you need. Remember: just because a Stafford loan is listed on your award letter doesn't mean you have to take it. In fact, you can decline it completely or simply accept only the amount you need. As long as you're in good academic standing, you can return to the financial aid office later in the year and borrow the amount you initially refused if you find you need it.

There are many free online programs that can help you calculate what your monthly loan payments will be depending on how much you borrow. One of the best is **www.finaid.com**.

The PLUS Loan

The Parent Loan for Undergraduate Students (PLUS) is an unsubsidized loan parents borrow on behalf of their dependent children enrolled in college as undergraduates. The PLUS loan may be used to pay any costs not covered by your other financial aid, all the way up to your total COA. Interest rates for the PLUS loan are capped at 9 percent, and there are no limits to how much your parents can borrow. Applying for a PLUS loan does not require you to complete the FAFSA, though this was stated incorrectly in some past Department of Education publications.

PLUS-ES

If you absolutely need additional funds to cover college costs, a PLUS loan is certainly a better option than a credit card or high-interest private loan. With interest rates reaching historic lows in 2004, the PLUS loan has become an even more attractive option for students with few other financial aid resources.

One additional factor that makes the PLUS loan more favorable than private loans is the fact that it, like Stafford and Perkins loans, may be consolidated into the Federal Consolidation Loan program, discussed in more detail later in this chapter.

Minuses

The PLUS loan is based on your parents' credit, so it is by no means a guaranteed safety net. If your parents are approved for a PLUS loan, you should be aware that the repayment policies are far less favorable than those of the Stafford or Perkins loan programs. There is only a sixty-day grace period, so repayment begins while you are still in school. Although some PLUS lenders now offer defer-ment of payments until after graduation, this results in a larger loan balance once payments do begin.

In almost every case, the unsubsidized Stafford loan is a better option than the PLUS loan. The interest rate is lower, the grace period is much longer, and approval does not depend on a credit check. However, as mentioned previously, dependent students are not eligible for any additional unsubsidized Stafford loan.

The PLUS loan has no limit, which some people con-sider one of its major drawbacks. Although the amount of your loan approval is determined by your parents' credit-worthiness, this might still allow a family to borrow tens of thousands of dollars, in addition to any Stafford or Perkins loans. Your debt can get very big, very fast. As with any loan, you should borrow only the minimum amount you need to cover your college costs—while con-tinuing to explore the free money that's out there.

Alternative or Private Loans

If you've maxed out your eligibility for Stafford and Perkins loans, and/or if your parents are denied a PLUS loan, there are many organizations that are perfectly willing to lend you the money you need for college. Unfortunately, these alternative or "private" loans don't have the same low-interest guarantees as federal student loans, and their fees are not limited by the Department of Education. Origination fees for these loans, for example, often exceed 10 percent. You should consider these alternatives only after you've exhausted all other sources of traditional financial aid.

If the alternative loan is an option you'd like to explore, one of the better programs is offered by the Educational Resources Institute, known among financial aid circles as the TERI loan. Visit www.teri.org for details about this nonprofit organization that has loaned money to more than one million students since 1985.

Consolidation Loans

Consolidation loans combine one or more of your student loans, usually Stafford, Perkins, or PLUS loans, to make it easier for you to repay them. If you consolidate your loans, you'll have to make only one monthly payment to one lender. You'll also be able to lock in a low interest rate, since Stafford and PLUS loans are variable rate loans. Consolidation loans also offer a diverse number of flexible repayment periods, from twelve to thirty years. Generally, you won't have to worry about consolidating your loans until you've graduated from college.

The Grace Period Loophole

If you are considering loan consolidation, you should be aware that timing is everything. Consolidation loan interest rates are based on the average of all the loans being consolidated. As mentioned earlier, interest rates for Stafford loans are actually 0.6 percent lower while you are still a student and during your grace period. This means that if you consolidate your loans before you graduate or before your grace period expires, your consolidation loan interest rate will be set at the lower rate. This 0.6 percent may

The Department of Education has compiled a great deal of resources for students interested in loan consolidation. Visit **www. loanconsolidation. ed.gov** for more information.

not seem like much now, but over the course of ten years, it can add up to hundreds—even thousands—of dollars in savings.

Consolidation Loan Drawbacks

If you decide to take advantage of the grace period loophole, keep in mind that once you consolidate your loans, you're responsible for making payments immediately. You'll lose any remaining months you may have had in your grace period. Also, any special loan forgiveness benefits offered by the Perkins loan will be lost once these loans are consolidated. Finally, even though consolidation loans offer extended repayment plans, the downside is that over the life of the loan, your total payments will be higher since you'll be paying more interest.

Emergency Loans

Many colleges have emergency or short-term loan programs for students who find themselves in a financial bind. Sometimes these loan programs are specifically designed for students who have yet to complete the FAFSA, and once the Stafford or Perkins loan money arrives, the balance of the emergency loan must be paid out of these funds.

Most major colleges have some sort of short-term loan program, and even much smaller institutions are able to offer emergency assistance. Tiny Clover Park Technical College in Tacoma, Washington, for instance, offers short-term aid through its college foundation that doesn't even have to be repaid. Make sure you check with both the college's financial aid office and the college's foundation, if one exists, for emergency financial aid options.

Forgiveness and Other Loan Benefits

As mentioned earlier, the Perkins loan may be partially forgiven under certain circumstances, such as if you serve in AmeriCorps*VISTA or the Peace Corps. Even PLUS and Stafford loans offer forgiveness in some situations, such as in the death or permanent disability of the student. Not all circumstances for loan forgiveness are so dire, however. There are plenty of loans designed to be forgiven and plenty of loan benefits available if you know where to look.

Indian Health Service Loan

The Indian Health Service (IHS), a division of the U.S. Department of Health and Human Services, has a great deal for health professionals willing to serve two years at IHS facilities across the country. IHS will pay up to $20,000 of your student loans. And since those loan payments are taxable, IHS will sweeten the deal by paying 20 percent of the taxes incurred as a result of your loan repayment. Visit **www.ihs.gov** and follow the "Jobs and Scholarships" link to find out more.

National Health Service Corps

Not to be outdone by fellow bureaucrats within Health and Human Services, the National Health Service Corps has a loan repayment program of its own for health professionals willing to serve in high shortage/low service areas for two to four years. In addition to receiving a salary, health professionals will receive up to $50,000 in loan repayment and up to 39 percent of any federal taxes accrued as a result of these payments. For more information, check out **nhsc.bhpr.hrsa.gov**.

Nurses Reinvestment Act

If you decide nursing is your life's calling, you should definitely dial into the Nurses Reinvestment Act, which will pay up to 60 percent of your approved student loans for serving two years in a critical shortage facility. You'll find an application and a list of FAQs at **bhpr.hrsa.gov/nursing/**.

Incentives to Teach

Many states offer loan repayment incentives to students in order to fill teaching positions. The Cal State University system (**www.calstate.edu/HR/FLP/**), for example, will provide up to $30,000 in forgivable loans to those who later obtain CSU faculty positions. In Chapter 6, "The State System," you'll also discover that most states have loan or scholarship incentives to cover local teaching needs, shortages among child care professionals, and/or gaps in fire/protection services.

AmeriCorps Benefits

If you decide to join an AmeriCorps national service program, there are three loan benefits for which you may be eligible. First, those who participate in AmeriCorps are usually eligible for loan forbearance during their term of service. Second, AmeriCorps will pay the loan interest that accrues for members who complete a full-time, year-long stint. Finally, AmeriCorps members can receive an educational allowance up to $9,450 in exchange for two years of national service, which can be used to repay Stafford, Perkins, and Federal Consolidation loans. These benefits won't hurt your financial aid eligibility. Neither the education award nor the money AmeriCorps contributes to paying your loan interest will be included when your EFC is calculated. Check out the AmeriCorps website, **www.americorps.org**, for details.

G

THE STATE SYSTEM

"Originally, I planned to study out of state. But when I saw how much financial aid I could get closer to home, I decided to earn my undergraduate degree here. With the money I'm saving, I'll be much better off when I go to grad school—out of state!"

Jean, 20

States don't always do a good job of promoting how much financial aid they can offer to local students. Texas alone offers up to $3 billion per year in total financial aid. California and New Jersey each budget nearly $1 billion for grants, loans, and work-study.

While the federal grant programs are based on need, many state awards are based on a combination of need and merit. Students who are ineligible for Pell Grants are sometimes very surprised to discover they've won a big pot of cash closer to home. You should actually be thankful the states don't know how to advertise their financial aid—the fewer people who know about this money, the better your chances of getting it yourself!

Do Your Homework . . .

Since information on state financial aid isn't always being plastered on bus windows or being written in the air with smoke, don't make the mistake of relying on your high school guidance counselor to know about all the state financial programs that exist. Even the sharpest guidance counselors sometimes miss the best of what's out there simply because state programs can change from year to year.

. . . And Do It Quickly

Just as with federal aid, state financial aid requires that you complete the FAFSA. The priority deadline for completing the FAFSA varies considerably from state to state, so be forewarned. Michigan and Rhode Island, for example, require that completed FAFSAs arrive at the financial aid office by March 1. Since processing a paper FAFSA for the first time can take up to six weeks, this means that in order to be absolutely sure you'll meet your state's financial aid deadlines, you should complete your paperwork in January.

State Scholarships

If you limit all your state scholarship research to the internet, you might not realize that individual states offer some of the best free ways to pay for college. Some of these scholarships cover full COA expenses for up to five years. But if you want to stay ahead of the game, you'll need to check with your state's higher education agency each year, since scholarship programs come and go depending on changes in political leadership and state budgets.

Merit Scholarships

As the name implies, states award merit scholarships based on student achievement. For example, any student in Mississippi who has a 3.5 GPA in high school and scores a 29 on the ACT may receive up to $2,500 per year for four years. Missouri residents, including home-schooled students, are eligible for a similar merit program, known as the Bright Flight scholarship, which awards up to $2,000 per year. Oklahoma's Academic Scholars Program offers students up to $5,500 per year to stay home and attend college in-state. The highly competitive Palmetto Fellowship offers South Carolina students even more: up to $6,700.

Don't let the term *merit* scare you off, even if you didn't exactly ace your PSATs. The definition of "student achievement" varies considerably from state to state. One of the best merit programs, the West Virginia Promise Scholarship, offers students who have a 3.0 GPA and score a 21 on the ACT a full-tuition scholarship to any in-state college or university. Arkansas rewards nontraditional students through its Second Effort scholarship, giving $1,000 to those who score in the top 10 percent on the GED.

Vocational Scholarships

In addition to scholarships based on merit, many states offer scholarships for students who are studying certain professional subjects or who are attending vocational/technical colleges. Approximately one out of every two applicants wins the generically named "Vocational

WWW Marks the Spot

Each state's higher education agency may be found online at **www. ed.gov/erod/** by clicking the "state/ territory" link.

These higher education agencies often sponsor free financial aid workshops that can give you the inside scoop on state financial aid programs.

10
STATE
Gold Mines

State money comes from many sources, including:

1

Merit scholarships

2

Vocational scholarships

3

Matching scholarships

4

Need-based grants

5

Out-of-state grants

6

Grad school assistance

7

Tuition reciprocity

8

State loans

9

Tax credits

10

Work-study

Scholarship" in Kansas for $500 each year. Want a degree in forestry wildlife or marine science? If you live in Louisiana, you need to know about the Rockefeller State Wildlife Scholarship, which awards $1,000 to sixty such students each year. And perhaps no state appreciates its future veterinarians as much as New Hampshire, which offers $12,000 scholarships to those students studying veterinary medicine. States offer scholarships for many other fields of study, usually in order to meet worker shortages or to support traditional industries.

Matching Scholarships

When you win a scholarship, you'll probably ask yourself, "Can things get any better?" The answer to that question just might be a resounding "Yes!" Some states will actually match the amount of your scholarship—which means you'll wind up with double the amount you started with. If you hail from Nebraska, for example, the Community Scholarship Foundation Program, administered by the state's Coordinating Commission for Postsecondary Education, might double the amount of your scholarship up to an additional $2,000. The New Hampshire Leveraged Incentive Grant Program is a merit-based scholarship program that is matched dollar for dollar by participating New Hampshire colleges.

State Grants

Most states offer some sort of grant assistance to its residents based on financial need. By and large, students who receive Pell Grants usually meet the state need-based grant requirements, but some states are even less stringent than the federal government. New York State's Tuition Assistance Program (TAP), for example, offers grant aid to dependent students whose families net as much as $80,000. This means that if you didn't receive

Private vs. Public

Don't assume that just because these scholarships are funded through the states that they're limited only to public colleges. Many of the state scholarship and grant programs offer larger awards for students attending private colleges, as a way of bridging the tuition gap between private and public institutions.

a Pell Grant, you might still be able to receive a need-based state grant. Home sweet home, indeed.

Need-Based Grants

As mentioned earlier, most state grants disappear quickly. If you want to receive a Frank O'Bannon Need-Based Grant to attend college in Indiana, for example, your FAFSA must be received no later than March 10. Just remember that all that extra on-time preparation will be well worth the effort. Washington State's Need Grant offers eligible students up to $4,650, $600 more than a Pell Grant. Arizona's LEAP grant is only $2,500, but since Arizona State University charges residents less than $2,500 for tuition, a little goes a long way. On the other end of the scale, California offers its residents up to $9,708 in Cal Grants. You snooze, you lose.

Nonresident Assistance

Do you love your state but want to live someplace else for the next four years? Some states won't hold you back. Vermont, in fact, offers its residents up to $9,100 to attend college either in-state or out-of-state. The DC Tuition Assistance Grant (DC TAG) allows District of Columbia residents to attend any public institution in the nation as though they were a resident of that state, by paying the difference between in-state and out-of-state tuition, up to $10,000 per year for five years.

Other Grants

States award other grant aid for a variety of reasons. Iowa offers a $1,200 vocational grant, which, unlike vocational scholarships, is based on need, not merit. Many states, including North Carolina, offer need-based grants specifically to students pursuing a two-year degree at a community or technical college. If you meet certain criteria and want to attend a private rather than a public college, Connecticut offers a specific grant for its residents to do so, up to $8,500 per year through the Independent College Student Grant Program. Tennessee offers a one-time grant for students who don't meet the requirements of its flagship HOPE Scholarship. If your parents earn less than $36,000 per year and you scored 860 on the SAT, you might wind up with an additional $2,000 grant to help see you through your first year of college.

Grad School Assistance

Unlike the federal government, many individual states offer grant and scholarship programs for those wishing to pursue graduate studies. Arkansas, for example, offers up to $7,500 for minority students who pursue a master's degree. Kansas encourages its graduate students to add a study abroad component to their curriculum through stipends averaging almost $2,500 with the James B. Pearson Fellowship program. In Ohio, the Regents Graduate/Professional Fellowship program awards up to $3,500 per year for two years of graduate study based on academic merit. If you want to pay for grad school, make sure you include state assistance in your financial aid strategy.

Residency

Have you ever noticed the difference between in-state and out-of-state tuition costs at public colleges and wondered, "Can't we all just get along?" Since public institutions of higher education generally receive much of their support from in-state tax dollars, out-of-state students will need to figure out how to bridge this tuition gap, which often exceeds $10,000 per year.

Gaining Residency

If you could gain state residency for a public college, all your problems would magically disappear. You'd pay lower tuition, you'd be eligible for all of that state financial aid, and you'd have a great excuse for learning a new set of state flowers, birds, mottos, and songs. Unfortunately, as anyone who has ever tried to gain state residency solely for the purpose of paying in-state tuition will admit, you might want to put those prospects on hold. Most state colleges understand that out-of-state students will try

Memorial Assistance

Several states have established memorial scholarships to assist those impacted by national tragedies. Oklahoma has created a fund to assist those affected by the Oklahoma City bombing, and both New York and New Jersey offer financial aid specifically for the victims of the September 11 attacks. If you are a relative of a police officer, firefighter, or soldier who died in the line of duty, you may be eligible for similar scholarships set up by many state higher education boards nationwide.

just about anything to become one of the natives, so they usually make the requirements fairly difficult to meet.

If you do decide to give residency a shot, make sure you check the residency requirements with the college or colleges you want to attend at least one year before the first day of classes. Most state schools require residency requirements to be in place for no fewer than 365 days before school begins. And if you start school as a nonresident, your chances of gaining residency afterward will be pretty slim.

Tuition Reciprocity

Many groups of states have agreements in place to benefit one another's students. These agreements, known as tuition reciprocity agreements, allow out-of-state students to pay tuition that is near what in-state students pay to attend publicly supported colleges and universities. For example, sixteen southern states are members of the Academic Common Market, sponsored by the Southern Regional Economic Board (**www.sreb.org**). If you are a resident of one of these states and wish to attend a public college in another member state, you may be eligible to pay the lower in-state tuition.

Another reciprocity agreement exists for fifteen western states through the Western Interstate Commission for Higher Education (**www.wiche.edu**). And Minnesota (**www.mhec.org**) has its own agreement in place with Wisconsin, North Dakota, South Dakota, and even the Canadian province of Manitoba. Many reciprocity agreements exist among particular schools, so if you decide to attend an out-of-state college, make sure you ask the financial aid office if any possibility exists for you to pay the lower in-state tuition rate without applying for residency.

Other State Assistance

States have put on their creativity caps when it comes to helping students pay for college. In addition to scholarships, grants, and tuition reciprocity, higher education commissions nationwide continuously create new programs you should know about.

State Loans

From Chapter 5, "The Loans," you know that the best federal loan goes by the name of Perkins. But depending on what you want to study, many individual states offer loans that beat the best federal lending programs in terms of interest rates, repayment plans, and forgiveness. For example, California will pay off up to $19,000 of your student loans if you decide to become a teacher. Through Pennsylvania's Agricultural Loan Forgiveness Program, you might be eligible to have up to $2,000 of your loan forgiven for each year you practice veterinary medicine or work on a family farm, up to $10,000. Massachusetts offers a no-interest loan for its students, up to $4,000. Many other states offer special loan deals for teachers, public servants, and health professionals.

State Tax Credits

A few states have even taken the enterprising step of helping students pay for college by offering tax credits. In South Carolina, students may claim a credit of 25 percent of their tuition, up to $850 per year. Depending on which college you attend in Michigan, you might be eligible for a $375 credit. And New York residents may qualify for a $400 tax credit for undergraduate tuition expenses.

State Work-Study

Though we'll discuss the benefits of work-study in more detail in Chapter 7, "The Other Aid," you should know

National Student Exchange

If you're curious about what college life outside your state is like, or if you always wanted to take a few courses in an obscure subject not offered at your in-state college, the National Student Exchange might be the thing for you. Visit **www.nse.org** for details.

that many states have their own pools of work-study funds available only to residents. In addition, many of these states offer additional incentives for work-study recipients. Many work-study positions may be structured as internships, which means that not only are you being paid, but you're also earning credit toward your degree. In addition, many of the best on-campus jobs are available only to work-study students.

There's More!

The Utah legislature created the New Century Scholarship program in order to award scholarships to high school students who complete the requirements of an associate's degree while still in high school. Texas actually offers a $1,000 tuition rebate to students who attempt no more than three semester credits beyond the minimum needed in their degree program (choose your electives carefully!). Kentucky has a program known as NAFTA-TAA (North American Free Trade Agreement Transition Adjustment Assistance), which assists students who have lost their jobs due to trade with Canada or Mexico. And Montana assists its students through a host of fee waiver programs, particularly for American Indians, senior citizens, and honorably discharged veterans.

This is only a sampling of the kinds of innovative state financial aid programs available. Be sure to do your research into your own state's programs. You can also get a weekly newsletter that will update you on new programs as they become available. Go to www.hewi.net, the Higher Education Washington, Inc. site, to sign up.

7

THE OTHER AID

"Finally he said, 'You've got a money problem. But that's not unusual. Almost everybody has a money problem. What you need is a job.'"

E. B. White
The Trumpet of the Swan

Think you know all your options for financial aid? Think again. Grants, scholarships, and loans are just the beginning—a little more digging will reveal even more ways to pay for college. If you're prepared to do a little work and get creative, the next four years might not be so hard on your wallet after all.

Work-Study

What does the term *work-study* mean to you? It probably conjures up images of students manning the information desk at the library, busily completing their homework for the next day, and this image is right on target. If work-study is part of your financial aid package, you'll be paid to work a limited number of hours each week, while you take classes. However menial the work may seem, work-study is a great way to pay for college.

Big Benefits

Work-study is usually part-time work, though in some cases it may be temporary full-time employment. You'll be paid by the university, and most jobs are on campus. Many students avoid work-study because they think they can find another part-time job with higher wages, and indeed, many nonwork-study jobs may pay better. However, work-study wages are not counted as income in the process used to calculate your EFC, which means that the money you earn is yours to keep. In other words, even if you do earn more money from your nonwork-study job, you may end up giving a big part of it to the government. If you remember from Chapter 3, "The Short Plan," the FAFSA assesses dependent student earnings up to 50 percent. Even with lower wages, work-study turns out to be a pretty good deal.

You'll find other benefits to work-study as well. Say, for example, you're majoring in biology and you find out about a great part-time job in the science lab. You might discover that only work-study students can apply. This happens a lot, and it makes sense: work-study students don't cost the university very much to hire. Typically, the federal government pays between 75 percent and 100 percent of work-study wages.

Because work-study students are a practically cost-free labor source, you're almost guaranteed some kind of campus employment if work-study is part of your financial aid package.

Nice Work If You Can Get It

Getting a work-study job is easy—but getting a work-study award in the first place can be quite difficult. Work-study is a campus-based program, just like the Supplemental Educational Opportunity Grant, which means it runs out quickly. If you want work-study, you should complete the FAFSA as soon as possible. (Be sure to answer "yes" to the question that asks, "In addition to grants, are you interested in 'work-study'?") By the way, just because you answer "yes" on the FAFSA doesn't mean you *must* accept the work-study award if you receive it.

Financial aid offices award work-study based on need, which adds to the difficulty of getting it—you have to have substantial need in order to receive work-study funds. However, the minimum EFC needed to qualify for work-study is typically much higher than for grants, so you might qualify for work-study even if you have too high an EFC to qualify for a Pell Grant or SEOG.

Cooperative Education

After you graduate and start looking for your first job, wouldn't it be great to have some relevant work experience to go along with your stellar GPA? Cooperative education programs, or "co-ops," provide exactly that. With a co-op, you'll have the chance to work full-time *and* study full-time, usually alternating by semester. Co-ops generally lengthen your undergraduate degree by one year.

Big Benefits

If you do a co-op, you'll get some great benefits. First, you'll get real-world work experience in your chosen field. Don't underestimate the value of coming out of college with a jump start on your resume! Even better, many companies hire their co-op students full-time after they

Trade-Offs

Work-study counts as a financial aid resource, which means it may reduce your other aid. Since work-study falls under the category of self-help aid, financial aid offices will typically reduce your loan amount rather than your grants or scholarships if your total financial aid package exceeds the COA. If you would prefer not to work, you might be able to increase your Stafford loan by declining work-study.

10
MORE WAYS
To Pay

1

Work-study

2

Cooperative education

3

Internships

4

Fee and tuition waivers

5

Competency-based education

6

Proficiency exams

7

Dual high school/ college programs

8

Early college prep programs

9

Community college articulations

10

Dual undergrad/ grad programs

graduate. By doing a co-op, you might eliminate your job search altogether. Co-ops also give you the chance to see if you've chosen the right path—there's no better way to evaluate your career choice than to get out there and see what it's like firsthand to work in the field.

You also get some great financial benefits from co-oping, and not just because most co-op jobs pay decent salaries. Some colleges think co-ops are so important that they'll waive your tuition for participating.

Work Colleges

Some schools take the co-op idea to the ultimate level: *every* student enrolled must participate. At some schools, such as Warren Wilson College in North Carolina, students can even be suspended for not working. But when you consider the financial aid benefits, school-related work seems like a pretty good deal. At Kentucky's Berea College, which is consistently rated among the top five colleges in the South, admitted students pay no tuition whatsoever. The same is true for Alice Lloyd College, also in Kentucky, as well as College of the Ozarks in Missouri.

Internships and More

A co-op isn't the only option for combining real-world work with your studies. Internships, practicums, and assistantships provide great financial aid benefits if you're willing to roll up your sleeves and get down to business. And, as always, the sooner you can start building your resume, the better.

Internships

Internships are credit-bearing, preprofessional jobs, either full- or part-time, that are related to your field of interest. An internship can provide you with real-life work experiences that translate into academic credit. In terms

"Pursuing an internship was the best decision I could have made. I earned a little bit of money, received college credit, and, most important, got a step up in my job search."

Alice, 21

10

CO-OP
Deals

The following schools are all members of the National Commission for Cooperative Education and offer scholarships to students who participate in co-op programs.

1   **Antioch College:** five $5,000 co-op scholarships, up to $20,000

2   **Drexel University:** ten $5,000 co-op scholarships, up to $25,000

3   **Johnson & Wales University:** ten $5,000 co-op scholarships, up to $20,000

4   **Kettering University:** ten $5,000 co-op scholarships, up to $20,000

5   **Long Island University, CW Post Campus:** four $5,000 co-op scholarships, up to $20,000

6   **Northeastern University:** ten $5,000 co-op scholarships, up to $25,000

7   **Pace University:** five $5,000 co-op scholarships, up to $25,000

8   **Rochester Institute of Technology:** five $5,000 co-op scholarships, up to $20,000

9   **University of Cincinnati:** five $5,000 co-op scholarships

10 **University of Waterloo (Canada):** five $5,000 co-op scholarships

of paying for college, the best internships offer decent wages, directly transferable credit, and other benefits, such as free housing.

Larger colleges often have a staff member who coordinates internship opportunities. At smaller schools, you may need to seek out internships on your own. Fortunately, the Internet is an easy way to seek out the better internship opportunities. But if a quality internship is in your future, you'll need to get started right away—paid internships can be highly competitive. Also, even if your college has an internship coordinator, you may have to complete a lot of paperwork in order to receive the college credit that makes this option such a great way of paying for college.

Practicums

Practicums, like internships, give you direct experience in your field of study. Practicums differ slightly from internships in that colleges usually treat them as ordinary classes and give you credit for completing them, whereas internships typically take place off campus and require written agreements so that the credits transfer. In terms of financial aid, practicums don't usually offer the same benefits as internships. In most cases, you won't receive any pay for your practicum experience, though many colleges offer some benefits. Case Western Reserve University, for example, does not charge tuition for students doing a practicum.

Assistantships

If you decide that getting a true college experience requires living in a dorm, you'll be happy to find that some students who live on campus get a great break on housing fees if they decide to become resident assistants. Resident assistants, or RAs, have long been maligned as the equivalent of dormitory police, ready to come

For a listing of colleges that offer free or reduced tuition in exchange for work, visit **www. workcolleges. org**.

Just about every major industry has an internship program of some kind, including— you guessed it— college financial aid (**www.interns. sfa.ed.gov**).

10
GREAT
Internships

The following internships offer great financial benefits and cover a variety of academic areas. Start your research early—competition is fierce.

1. **Environmental Studies:** You can find environmental conservation internships in abundance at www.sca-inc.org. Fittingly, many of these internships are renewable.

2. **Journalism:** Think you're the next Woodward or Bernstein? You'll have a better idea after completing a summer internship at the Washington Post (**www.wash-post.com**). This internship is highly competitive and well paid at $825/week.

3. **High-Tech:** Dude, you're gettin' a job. At $480/week, Dell internships provide paid experience in the computer business.

4. **Law Enforcement:** The FBI Internship offers you a salary of $390/week, lunch with the director of the FBI . . . and a chance to explain those parking tickets.

5. **Health:** The National Institutes of Health offer competitive, paying internships ($1,900/month) in areas such as biomedical research.

6. **Philanthropy:** Want to make a career of giving back to local communities? The Ford Foundation hires full-time interns. Besides a $35,000/year salary, you'll also gain the experience of getting to know the inner mechanics of private philanthropy.

7. **Engineering/Math:** Students within two years of graduating from an engineering, math, or physical science program may apply for $4,500 ATT internships.

8. **Art:** Perhaps your parents weren't exactly thrilled when you announced you'd be majoring in art history. Their attitude might change when you tell them you've won a $2,250 Cloisters internship at the Metropolitan Museum of Art.

9. **Business:** Yes, you can get free housing and pay based on experience. An internship at Abbot Laboratories (**www.abbott.com**) awaits.

10. **Science:** There's nothing weird about a science internship at NASA (**www.nasa-jobs.nasa.gov**).

knocking whenever your stereo gets loud enough to actually hear the music. But great responsibility also brings great rewards. That resident assistant who just told you to turn down the volume very likely pays *nothing* for room and board.

In addition to resident assistantships, some colleges offer teaching or research assistantships to outstanding undergraduate students. A good example is Brown's Undergraduate Teaching and Research Assistantship (UTRA), which comes with a $1,000 stipend and reduces the amount of self-help aid (loans, work-study) that you have to carry. Colleges generally reserve teaching and research assistantships for graduate students, but it never hurts to ask if they'll make an exception.

Waivers

As mentioned earlier, colleges can waive your tuition for various reasons (see Chapter 4, "The Free Money"). There's more good news: colleges can waive other costs as well. Remember that the COA includes tuition *and* fees—and at some schools, these fees can be substantial. Even having one fee waived can make a difference. During the college years, every dollar counts.

Killer Fees

You might think long distance phone companies take the grand prize when it comes to charging customers miscellaneous fees—but wait until you get your first college tuition bill. Colleges often charge students numerous fees, in some cases ten or more, for things like student activities, technology, health insurance, and laboratory usage. Did you register late for class? You'll need to pay the late enrollment fee. Do you want to change courses after the semester begins? Don't forget to pay your late change of registration fee.

Colleges have gotten creative in gaining revenue through fees, with some colleges having separate fees for programs that seem virtually identical. Try not to lose it when you find out your college charges fees for student recreation, student activities, *and* the student union. Unfortunately, even if you don't participate in any of these programs, you'll still receive a bill and be required to pay for them.

From Fee to Free

Being a thrifty college student, you need to know how to get out of paying some of these fees. Fortunately, colleges do take special circumstances into consideration. For example, many schools waive the application fee if you have substantial financial need. Entrance exam fees, such as for the SAT, are also quite commonly waived for students with evidence of financial need. Does one of your relatives actually work for the college? If so, you might be eligible for tuition or fee waivers based on this fact alone.

Check with the financial aid office, bursar's office, or student accounts office early on to see what, if any, waivers your college might offer. In addition to waiving application and testing fees, some schools will waive health fees if you can prove you have outside insurance. Some schools even allow you to waive activity fees if you agree to also waive regular access to those services. Just as with your telephone bill, don't be afraid to question whether or not you should be paying for every charge that's listed.

College Credit

A riddle for you: what is just like money, can get you stuff just like money, but in fact isn't really money? That, as any department store clerk will tell you, is credit. When it comes to paying for college, credit trumps cash in the financial aid game. And as you'll see below, you have more than one ace in the hole when it comes to winning college credit.

Experience-Based Credit

In response to a growing number of nontraditional students (that is, students who don't fall between the ages of eighteen and twenty-two), many colleges offer credit to students based on their real-life experiences. At the Evergreen State College in Olympia, Washington, for example, you can earn up to 45 credits for the equivalent of a year's worth of life or work experience, all of which count toward the 180 credits needed for a bachelor's degree. Fordham University offers 32 credits toward a degree.

One thing about experience-based credit remains constant, at both large public schools like Indiana or small liberal arts colleges like Antioch: many students have no idea that these programs exist.

Evergreen calls this type of program "Prior Learning from Experience," while Penn State prefers "Portfolio Assessment." Other colleges use the phrase "Competency-Based Education." Regardless of the name, getting credit for life or work experience typically involves enrolling in a one- to three-hour course that walks you through the process of recording and documenting your experiences in academic terms. You'll then submit the result, which can be a portfolio of past work, a written narrative, or another form, for credit evaluation.

Certificated Learning

Colleges have also begun to recognize the professional certificates and licensures many students hold. Perhaps you earned your pilot's license or a certificate as a Microsoft Office Specialist. If so, be sure and talk with the admissions or registrar's office to see if those certificates might translate into academic credit. After all, education comes in many shapes and sizes. You might as well turn yours into dollar signs.

Why exactly are credits better than cash? Because credits, unlike traditional forms of financial aid, don't show up in your EFC, even though they're often worth thousands of dollars. And since these credits don't affect your EFC, they won't reduce the total amount of traditional financial aid and scholarships you might receive. Credit really *is* better than cash. American Express should look no further for its new slogan.

Proficiency Exams

There's nothing like a test to strike fear into a student's heart. But consider this: you can potentially test your way out of thousands of dollars in college tuition. Many colleges will allow you to substitute exam scores for full college credit—credit that can help you graduate early and on budget.

CLEP

For more information about both CLEP and AP exams, visit the College Board website, **www. collegeboard. com**.

The College Level Examination Program (CLEP) offers you the chance to earn credit just by taking a test. In fact, the College Board reports that 2,900 colleges offer credit to students who successfully take the CLEP exam every year. Each college will have different rules about which tests you can take, what your minimum score needs to be in order to receive credit, and what fees are added onto the $55 the College Board charges for each CLEP exam.

Since college tuition far exceeds these test fees, each successful CLEP exam you take is just like getting a minis-cholarship. For example, let's say you'll be attending the Rochester Institute of Technology. Since each credit at RIT costs $468, receiving just ten CLEP credits for two tests can save you $4,500. Who's afraid of tests now?

AP

"I wound up saving almost $20,000 by graduating early. It was a lot of work, but so is an extra year of college."

Damian, 23

If your high school offers Advanced Placement (AP) cours-es, you'll have the chance to take another proficiency examination for which you can receive college credit. Just as with CLEP, rules for how many credits you can receive vary from college to college, but with more than thirty different AP courses available, opportunities for credit abound.

Before you begin your junior year of high school, talk with your guidance counselor to see what, if any, AP courses your school offers. Although your school may not offer fourteen AP courses like Medford High in Massachusetts, there's a good chance it offers one or two.

IB

Some high schools participate in something called the International Baccalaureate (IB) Programme, which offers a series of college preparatory classes. If your high school offers these classes, you can enroll in them just like any other class, and you'll still fulfill all the requirements you need to earn a regular high school diploma. But by taking and passing IB classes, you'll also earn an IB diploma that is recognized by many colleges both in the United States and abroad. Like CLEP and AP, IB participants can also take examinations that colleges will then evaluate for credit transfer.

If you have participated in the IB program or have an IB diploma, you might want to visit the IB website at **www.ibo.org** to search for colleges that will grant you credit.

Still More Tests

In addition to CLEP, AP, and IB, some colleges accept numerous other kinds of proficiency examination credits. For instance, most larger schools allow incoming students to test out of basic coursework through institutional proficiency exams offered only at the school. Taking advantage of this opportunity can shorten the time it takes to graduate, often by an entire semester, which can substantially reduce your long-term college costs.

When it comes to commercial proficiency examinations, the CLEP and AP exams find themselves in crowded company. More and more schools offer credit for ACT PEP (Proficiency Examination Program), ECE (Excelsior College Examinations), and CEEB (College Entrance Examination Board) tests. Ask your college registrar if they accept any of these results for college credit.

High School Strategies

If you want to enter college with some credits under your belt but don't want to take AP or IB courses, you have a few options at your disposal. Be aware, however, that the following programs aren't for everyone. High school is hard enough as it is without adding college to the mix.

TEST-FOR-CREDIT
Programs

1

CLEP: College Level Examination Program

2

AP: Advanced Placement

3

IB: International Baccalaureate

4

ACT PEP: ACT Proficiency Examination Program

5

ECE: Excelsior College Examinations

6

CEEB: College Entrance Examination Board

7

INSTITUTIONAL PROFICIENCY EXAMINATION: offered by individual schools

8

PONSI: New York Regents National Program on Noncollegiate Sponsored Instruction

9

ACE CCRS: American Council on Education College Credit Recommendation Service

10

DANTES: Defense Activity for Nontraditional Education Support

Running Start

If your secret fantasy involves being an average Joe by day, superhero by night, Jump Start might be just your thing. More and more, colleges are allowing high school students to take classes on their campuses that will later apply toward a degree. Some schools, such as Montana Tech, offer tuition discounts to participants. The state of Wisconsin takes this idea a step further. Under the Youth Options program, high school juniors and seniors can take courses at any University of Wisconsin institution, any Wisconsin community college, any Wisconsin technical college, and even some private colleges free of charge, upon approval by the local school board. In Georgia, the Accel Program, formerly known as Postsecondary Options, pays the tuition for eligible high school juniors and seniors who want to earn college credit. In Washington State, the Running Start program has for years offered students the ability to earn an associate degree while still in high school.

The catch to any of these programs, of course, is that all this extra studying can be demanding. Trying to pass both a college course and your regular high school classes can be a great way to get a head start on college—or a good way of getting in over your head.

Summer U.

Overwhelmed by the idea of taking high school and college classes at the same time? You have another option: summer school. Many colleges now allow students to earn credit in the summers following their junior and senior years of high school. You've already discovered that working during the summer can be hazardous to your financial aid health—summer school at a college might be the best medicine.

Keep in mind, however, that as a high school student you are ineligible for any federal financial aid. This means that unless your state or school board offers to pay your way, your tuition will be the same as that of any regularly admitted college student. In addition, admission requirements for high school students wishing to attend regular college courses tend to be very stringent.

TRIO

Depending on your background, you may qualify for participation in a federal program known as TRIO. TRIO began with three programs in the late 1960s as part of the War on Poverty. For the last forty years, TRIO has provided a wide range of services to first-generation, low-income, and/or disabled students, making college more accessible. As with the federal financial aid programs, TRIO is administered by the U.S. Department of Education.

This federal program issues grants to colleges and universities who then use that money to help high school students from disadvantaged backgrounds achieve their higher-education dreams. Talent Search and Upward Bound, two of TRIO's eight programs, target high school students. In addition to providing services such as tutoring, mentoring, academic preparation, financial aid counseling, and career exploration, TRIO offers financial aid assistance such as grants, scholarships, and work-study. Contact your prospective college to find out if they have TRIO programs and if you qualify.

GEAR UP

Many states participate in another federal college readiness program known as GEAR UP (Gaining Early Awareness & Readiness for Undergraduate Programs). In addition to eligibility for GEAR UP college scholarships, participants gain access to college and career counseling, test prep and financial aid advice, and a host of other services meant to help students succeed. Contact your high school or middle school counselor to see if your school participates and if you meet the eligibility requirements. Or visit the GEAR UP website for more information: www. ed.gov/programs/gearup.

Community College Strategy

Nothing beats a great return on a small investment. Community and technical college students have long held this as their mantra—and with good reason. Students at two-year colleges are turning their associate degrees into bachelor's degrees. And (all together now!) saving a whole lot of money in the process.

2 + 2 = $40,000

The logic seems simple enough. You spend two years at a community college to earn an associate degree. Theoretically, if each of those credits transfers to a four-year school, you'll need only two more years to earn a bachelor's degree. Not surprisingly, many colleges have begun to put this theory into practice. Referred to as a "2 + 2" program, it is an agreement between a two-year college and a four-year college that allows students with associate degrees to be granted junior status at the four-year school.

The benefits aren't limited to public universities. Whitworth College in Spokane, Washington, for example, participates in what they call an "Upside-Down" program, whereby community college students can receive full credit for their two-year degree. Since they are guaranteed junior standing when they enter a four-year school, this means they'll complete a bachelor's degree in only two more years. So if you begin your studies at Walla Walla Community College (total two-year tuition: $4,300) and finish a bachelor's program at Whitworth (tuition for junior and senior years: $41,960), you'll have saved $37,660 on your diploma.

Another Degree Option

Getting a great deal on a college degree doesn't apply only to undergrads. Sure, turning an associate degree into a bachelor's is a great way to save on college tuition. But what if you could turn that bachelor's degree into a master's?

Buy Four, Get One Free

Many schools now offer the option of allowing students to combine undergraduate and graduate degrees, at a considerable savings. At Lehigh University in Pennsylvania, education students can enter a program that

Some community and technical colleges form "articulation agreements" with universities so their students will have an easier time transferring and eventually graduating with a bachelor's degree. For a list of community/technical colleges who have developed national articulation agreements, visit the League for Innovation website, **www.league.org.**

allows them to earn a master's degree just by adding one more year to their undergraduate study. It's called the B.A./M.Ed. 5th Year Program, and it can offer significant savings to students interested in grad school, particularly if you recall that grad students do not qualify for any federal Pell or SEOG grants.

These "5th Year Master's" programs are a growing trend in higher education and are not limited to any one field of study. Carnegie Mellon offers a 5th Year Master's program for computer science majors. Vanderbilt has 5th Year Master's programs for a variety of fields, including human resources, organizational leadership, and community development. University of Virginia students can enroll in 5th Year Master's programs in biology, chemistry, math, psychology, and other science fields.

A Tale of Two Uncles

As you've seen, the wondrous world of financial aid involves much more than the old stand-bys of grants, scholarships, and loans. Here are two more institutions—uncles, if you will—that are willing to pay your way in exchange for your services or as a way of benefiting from your future success.

Uncle Sam

One of the better-known sources of financial aid, the U.S. military certainly puts its fair share of students through college. Students interested in attending a regular college might be interested in the Reserve Officers Training Corps (ROTC), which provides tuition expenses and a $100 monthly stipend. ROTC requires that participants serve in the armed forces after graduation.

Service academies provide tuition free of charge to students. These colleges are highly selective and also require five years of service in the military, but if you're interested in military service and gaining a college degree for free, there's really no better option.

There are four service academies:
1. The U.S. Military Academy (West Point, New York)
2. The U.S. Naval Academy (Annapolis, Maryland)
3. The U.S. Air Force Academy (Colorado Springs, Colorado)
4. The U.S. Coast Guard Academy (New London, Connecticut)

My Rich Uncle

If you don't feel like you're Uncle Sam's favorite niece or nephew, there might be someone else willing to help you out. MyRichUncle.com represents a unique trend in higher education: student sponsorships. Student sponsorships essentially partner college students with those who want to invest in their future. MyRichUncle.com provides you with the money you need to go to college, and in return you repay that loan with a percentage of your future income. Not everyone who applies for a student sponsorship will succeed, but for those who do, it can serve as a more manageable alternative to traditional student loans.

3

THE OFFER

"The silly boy could not hide the joy he felt at what he supposed was so good an offer, and the bargain was struck at once. The cow was thus exchanged for a few paltry beans."

From "Jack and the Beanstalk"
Anonymous

Now that you know all the basics of financial aid, you have to understand the anatomy of a financial aid offer, how an offer is made, and how you can improve it. You need to be able to separate fact from fiction: there are a lot of rumors out there about how to negotiate a better award.

10 Ways to Get More

Get ready: there are ten basic ways to get to a better financial aid offer. A few secrets do spice things up, but you might be pleasantly surprised to find out that the process is actually fairly simple. It all begins with getting a head start on the competition.

1. Beat the Deadlines

There's no way around it: the most effective way to maximize your financial aid award is to act quickly. You'll receive the best offer possible only if you complete your paperwork correctly and on time.

Act Now

Admissions officers at both public and private colleges want you to make your decision sooner rather than later. After all, the sooner they fill their classes, the more time they have to enjoy summer vacation. Once you've decided which colleges you'll apply to, make a list of each school's admissions and financial aid deadlines, including any deadlines for institutional scholarships.

Tax Time

To meet all the financial aid deadlines, you and your parents will probably need to estimate your income tax information, since most businesses wait until the last week of January before mailing W-2 forms. Estimating your prior year income information is perfectly acceptable—just be sure to complete the tax forms as soon as possible. Financial aid offices select many students for verification to make sure their estimates match their actual earnings, and those students must provide their prior year's income tax returns and still meet the priority deadline. Completing your tax returns as soon as possible will help you at award time.

Complete the Process

A bit of advice: don't focus so intensely on financial aid applications that you neglect the admissions process. Your strategy is to receive award letters from as many colleges as possible so you can shop around for the best deal. In order to do this, you need to understand that the admissions process is inextricably linked to the financial aid process. As in financial aid, applications for admission can sometimes go awry, and, unfortunately, most financial aid offices will not process your financial aid until after you've been admitted.

2. Choose Help Wisely

Though you can learn (and are learning) the basics of financial aid, you and your parents probably don't consider yourselves experts, and you might be tempted to look for expertise in the form of a financial aid consultant. Fortunately, financial aid consultants are easily found. Unfortunately, they face absolutely no licensing requirements. They need no minimum experience, no degree, and no record of success. You need to be a wise consumer.

Who Needs 'Em?

Students generally look for a consultant because of lack of knowledge and lack of time. Those who seek out consultants because they feel they lack knowledge often discover they've wasted a lot of money. All the information you need to maximize your financial aid starts on page one of this book. In fact, if you spy on your financial aid consultant in the middle of the night, you'll very likely see him or her reviewing the contents of a guide like this one.

But if you don't have the time to dedicate to your own financial aid future, a financial aid consultant *may* be worth the cost. The cost could range anywhere from $100

"We hired a financial aid consultant who guaranteed I'd receive financial aid. But all he did was complete my FAFSA, which I could have done on my own for free. And because I was offered a student loan, the consultant won't return my $1,000 fee."

Rebecca, 20

10

CONSULTANTS
To Avoid

Avoid consultants who:

1 Guarantee financial aid success. Virtually every student, if they have need, can get a PLUS loan or unsubsidized Stafford loan without a consultant.

2 Recommend that you hide your assets. This is illegal.

3 Claim that all financial aid offers are negotiable. This is untrue.

4 Are unprofessional, unkempt, or patronizing.

5 Recommend that you overestimate your income. They do this to create the illusion that they were able to lower your EFC by correcting your Student Aid Report.

6 Are difficult to reach. A disconnected number or a P.O. box is a bad sign.

7 Charge more than $1,000. There comes a point where the costs start outweighing the benefits.

8 Promise refunds. Refunds in the financial aid consultancy field are gimmicks—make them prove they've ever actually refunded someone's money.

9 Have experience mainly in financial advising. Financial advisors often give recommendations that are counterproductive to financial aid.

10 Are unwilling to sign your FAFSA, which is a requirement of any professional who assists you with it.

to simply help you fill out the FAFSA to upwards of $1,000 for a comprehensive consultation. So if you really want to get the best offer possible by employing the services of a financial aid consultant, there's even more homework to do.

What to Look For

If financial aid consultants were as useful as tax consultants, you could probably name one or two reputable firms off the top of your head. However, there is no financial aid equivalent to H&R Block. Most financial aid consultants are individuals who work out of their homes as independent contractors, often supplementing their business with other kinds of private consulting. If you're determined to hire one, ask the following questions to make sure you're getting the most for your money:

- Does the consultant have any experience as a financial aid administrator? If not, there's not much chance he or she really knows what goes on behind the scenes.

- Does the consultant have a history of success helping other families? You could call a local financial aid office to see if they've had any complaints about the consultant you've identified.

- Does the consultant display a depth of knowledge regarding both in-state and out-of-state financial aid? Don't be afraid to use all the acronyms and technical language you find in this guide during your meeting. If the consultant is unfamiliar with these terms, he or she is probably not qualified enough to serve you well.

3. Ace the Forms

Missing financial aid deadlines is the biggest mistake a student can make—and filling out forms incorrectly isn't far behind. With more than one hundred questions, the FAFSA has left a long list of victims in its wake. Since maximizing your financial aid award depends on getting everything right, think of the following information as your lifejacket.

Internet to the Rescue

Now that the Department of Education introduced online applications, avoiding mistakes is easier. In fact, completing the FAFSA online actally

KILLER
FAFSA Mistakes

1

Mistyping your social security number

2

Leaving blanks

3

Not reporting untaxed income in Worksheets A and B

4

Underreporting exempt income in Worksheet C

5

Using a nickname

6

Answering "No" to work-study or loans, thinking it will qualify you for more grants

7

Not counting yourself in household size

8

Reporting taxes withheld instead of taxes paid

9

Not including stepparents' information

10

Not providing signatures

eliminates two of the biggest problems: time and accuracy. Filing the online FAFSA is up to two weeks faster than filling out a paper FAFSA, and the online FAFSA also includes several safeguards that help prevent the most common mistakes. If you leave an answer blank, for example, the online version won't let you continue until you've answered the question. You should make every effort to complete the FAFSA online at **www. fafsa.ed.gov**.

Financial aid consultants make frequent use of the Federal Student Aid Information Center, a toll free hotline provided by the Department of Education. Direct your questions to 1-800-4-FED-AID.

The PIN

You can't complete the FAFSA before January 1, but you can and should start the process as soon as possible. When you submit the FAFSA online, the last step is either to submit a signature page or a PIN (Personal Identification Number). Sending in a signature page after you complete your FAFSA can take up to ten days to receive and process, whereas your PIN can be processed the very next day. That nine-day span might mean the difference between campus-based financial aid or more loans. Visit **www.pin. ed.gov** to request your PIN and stay ahead of the curve.

The PROFILE

The College Board CSS/Financial Aid PROFILE, used by several hundred schools to supplement the FAFSA, may also be completed online. To start the process, go to **profileonline.collegeboard.com** and register, which will set you back a cool $5. You may want to be choosy about where you send the PROFILE: the College Board charges $18 for each school. Be careful not to list a school that doesn't accept the PROFILE, since you'll just be throwing away your cash.

School Forms

Each college has its own financial aid form, most of which are straightforward. Filling out this form is a great opportunity for you to start establishing a relationship with your financial aid office. Simply call the office—or, better yet, visit if possible—and ask what mistakes students typically make on the institutional financial aid forms. You might just meet a particularly helpful financial aid counselor who could help you many times down the road.

4. Check Your SAR

Maximizing your financial aid award means staying one step ahead of everyone else, so you should review your Student Aid Report (SAR) as soon as you receive it. If you complete the FAFSA online, you'll receive your SAR up to four weeks sooner than if you complete a paper FAFSA. The SAR basically summarizes the answers from your FAFSA and provides you with your EFC, which tells colleges what the federal government expects you and your family to pay for college.

SAR Adjustment

Most students and their parents think their EFC is too high, and in a few cases, an adjustment may be possible. First, you should check your SAR to make sure you've submitted accurate information, including family size (did you include yourself?), income (if you've completed your taxes since submitting the FAFSA, has anything changed?), and personal information (if you're twenty-four, does the SAR list you as an independent?).

If you do find mistakes on your SAR, you can now make corrections online at fafsa.ed.gov, even if you completed a paper FAFSA. Making corrections online takes far less time than submitting changes through the mail, and you'll receive an immediate confirmation number verifying that your corrections have been received. Instant gratification in the world of financial aid—who knew?

No Time to Panic

You may not receive your SAR as soon as you expect. Don't panic: a delay can occur for many reasons. If your SAR doesn't arrive within a reasonable amount of time, you can call the federal processor to find out why, at 1-800-4-FED-AID.

Verification

On your SAR, you might notice an asterisk next to your EFC. If so, you've been selected for a process known as verification. (See Chapter 1, "The Process," for more details.) Being selected for verification doesn't mean you're in any kind of trouble, but you need to act fast. The financial aid office will ask you to submit copies of your relevant financial information, which will probably include a copy of your and your parents' federal income tax returns. Depending on why you were selected for verification, you may also need to submit copies of your birth certificate, marriage license, social security card, or other documents. Just follow the instructions given to you by the financial aid office as quickly as possible.

5. Appeal

The FAFSA is a one-size-fits-all kind of form, which means that it probably doesn't fit *anyone* just right—kind of like those gigantic T-shirts that could presumably fit both a linebacker and a baby. The Department of Education recognizes that since every student is different, financial aid administrators should have some leeway in making changes that could benefit you if you have unusual circumstances. This leeway is called professional judgment.

Professional Judgment (PJ)

If you have any unusual financial or personal circumstances, you should report them to your financial aid office. For example, you should let the office know if you have high medical expenses or if a parent has recently lost a job. Sometimes the FAFSA won't provide an adequate picture of your particular situation, in which case professional judgment may be used to changed how your need is calculated. Call or visit the financial aid office directly to find out what forms you'll need to report your circumstances. You'll probably need to submit a letter along with any written documentation that supports your claims.

Be sure you present your case in a clear and professional manner. As the instructions to the FAFSA state, the financial aid administrator's professional judgment decision is final and cannot be appealed to the U.S. Department of Education.

Must-Haves for a PJ Appeal

- **The form:** Every college has its own form for making a PJ appeal. Make sure you get the right form and follow the instructions exactly as they're written.

- **The procedure:** Financial aid administrators are sticklers for detail. If the form requires you to put two copies of everything in a manila envelope, don't give one copy in a file folder and assume they'll make an exception for the ultra-deserving you.

- **The time:** No matter how well you present your case, there are some things a financial aid administrator cannot override once you've submitted your FAFSA, as in cases of marriage. If you think you'll need to file an appeal, consult the financial aid office *before* filing your aid application.

- **The reasons:** PJ decisions can be granted for some, but not all, financial aid decisions. Dependency is one of just a few issues that can be affected by a PJ decision. Others might include adjustments to your family size, your COA, and even your available income.

- **The attitude:** Blaming your money problems on the financial aid advisor won't get you very far. Always stay calm and professional.

- **The evidence:** PJ requires that financial aid administrators support their decisions with adequate documentation. Adequate documentation is rarely handwritten and almost never written on cocktail napkins. A much better choice would be to submit all supporting documents on typewritten letterhead, or, in the case of unusual expenses, copies of items such as receipts or bills.

- **The strategy:** Talking to other students who have had successful PJ appeals is a great way to figure out what strategies might work for you.

- **The shoes:** If you have to come in for a hearing to determine your PJ status, make sure you dress professionally. It will show you're taking the process seriously.
- **The back-up plan:** The initial appeal didn't work? Even though the financial aid administrator's decision is final, there are others higher up on the food chain who may want to help you realize your dream of a higher education. A carefully written letter to the vice president for student affairs might do the trick.
- **The follow-up:** Successful or not, too few students realize the stress and anguish that financial aid administrators go through in making decisions that have life-altering consequences for students. A thank-you note goes a long way. In your next three years of college, you'll probably need the financial aid administrator's help again down the road.

Reasons to Appeal

The Department of Education lists the following as possible reasons for filing an appeal:

- Tuition expenses at an elementary or secondary school
- Unusual medical or dental expenses not covered by insurance
- A family member who recently became unemployed
- Changes in income or assets that may affect your eligibility for financial aid

Don't let this list limit you, however, and don't give up if your first appeal is rejected, especially if you think your reasons are legitimate and you have adequate evidence to back up your claims. If necessary, submit a second appeal to the financial aid director or even the dean of student services. Many students have successfully won appeals by being persistent.

How often do professional judgment decisions result in additional financial aid? A 2001 survey by the National Association of Student Financial Aid Administrators (**www.nasfaa. org**) found that professional judgment decisions led to an increase in total financial assistance in nearly half of all cases (48 percent, to be exact).

Act Quickly

If you're going to appeal, do it quickly. Even if the financial aid office makes a PJ decision in your favor, if the decision occurs after the campus-based aid has already been disbursed to other students, your additional financial aid may be limited to loans.

6. Understand the Letter(s)

At long last, you can take a breather and wait for your award letters to arrive in the mail. But when they finally do come, will you have enough of an understanding to choose which one is right for you? Award letters are as varied as the schools that produce them. However, each one should contain the same basic information, and the key to shopping for the best award lies in comparing these basics.

The Basics

Each award letter should tell you:

- Your total COA, ideally broken down into tuition, room/board, fees, and other expenses
- Your EFC, sometimes broken down into both your contribution and your parents' contribution
- Your total award, broken down by quarter or semester, and with a name or description of each award
- Instructions on how to proceed next, including an option to decline all or part of each award

The Letter

Sample College
Office of Student Financial Aid

Academic Year:

Date:

Student ID:

Your Name

Your Address

Your City, State Zip + 4

Award	Fall	Spring	Total Accept/ Decline
Pell Grant	$1,200	$1,200	$2,400
Supplemental Educational Opportunity Grant	$500	$500	$1,000
Sylvania Scholarship	$500	$500	$1,000
State Need Grant	$850	$850	$1,700
Federal Work Study	$1,000	$1,000	$2,000
Perkins Loan	$1,000	$1,000	$2,000
Stafford Subsidized Loan	$1,313	$1,312	$2,625
PLUS Loan for Parents	$2,887	$2,888	$5,775
Totals:	**$9,250**	**$9,250**	**$18,500**

Expected Family Contribution:	Student:	$1,200
	Parent:	$500
Total:		**$1,700**
Cost of Attendance:	Fall:	$9,250
	Spring:	$9,250
Total:		**$18,500**

Please sign the award letter and return to the Office of Student Financial Aid

Signature: _____ Date: _____

Making Sense of It All

In the above example, $12,725 of the aid is need-based, including $2,000 for work-study and $2,625 for subsidized loans. The remaining $5,775 takes the form of a nonneed-based PLUS loan. However, only $6,100 of the total award comes in the form of free aid, meaning that in order to cover costs, the student will likely need to incur some amount of educational loan debt.

The amount of debt that you will incur should be one of the key factors in determining which award will work for you.

7. Know the Ratio

What award letters *don't* tell you can be very important: the gift aid to self-help ratio. You learned about this ratio in Chapter 4, "The Free Money," and know that this is how colleges determine how much of your award will be in the form of grants/scholarships and how much will be in the form of loans and work-study. The best awards will be heavier on the gift aid side, and your job is to determine what, if any, exceptions can be made.

When Ratios Go Bad

The first exception concerns outside scholarships. Say, for example, that after receiving your award letter you discover you've won an outside scholarship worth $5,000. You must report this scholarship to the financial aid office as required by the Department of Education, and once you do report it, you may very likely find that your overall out-of-pocket expenses remain the same. This is one of those cruel facts of financial aid life that frustrate countless students each year. Instead of replacing your loans or work-study, you might find that the financial aid office has merely reduced your other institutional scholarship.

Not every college has the same gift aid to self-help ratio, which is why applying to several different colleges is so important. Although most colleges will tell you they won't bargain, this area may be one of the exceptions. Some colleges might be willing to adjust the ratio in the event that you've won outside financial assistance. After all, many of these scholarships, such as the National Merit Finalist Award, also boost the school's reputation. In fact, some schools will actually *reward* you for your outside scholarships, ratio or no ratio.

8. Negotiate

Talk to ten different financial aid administrators and you'll get ten different answers to the question of whether or not financial aid offices really do negotiate awards. At one end of the spectrum are colleges like

Carnegie Mellon, that have explicit language in their financial aid policies inviting students to submit better offers from competing schools. At the other end are a group of twenty-eight colleges, led by Duke University, that have banded together to completely eliminate the tug-of-war over student financial aid awards. Called the 568 Presidents' Group and named after the Improving America's Schools legislation, these colleges believe that years of negotiating practices have compromised the true intent of need-based financial aid.

In 2001, the presidents of these colleges signed an agreement known as the Consensus Approach to Need Analysis. This agreement essentially tells prospective students, "Take your haggling elsewhere." Other colleges in this group include MIT, Notre Dame, Rice, Stanford, Yale, and Georgetown.

Although most other colleges fall somewhere in between, talk to virtually any financial aid administrator about bargaining and you'll likely be met with a sigh and a rolling of the eyes. Studies by the National Association of Student Financial Aid Administrators back this up. In a 2001 survey by the National Association of Student Financial Aid Administrators (**www.nasfaa.org**), only 2 percent of colleges nationwide stated that they would be willing to change a financial aid award based on packages offered by other institutions.

Negotiate What You Can . . .

Regardless of policy, all financial aid offices have some leeway in adjusting your award, but this leeway rarely has anything to do with competing offers. Consider outside scholarships. If you are applying to two colleges, one that applies your outside scholarship toward your self-help aid first and one that applies it toward your gift aid, let the college know that this will affect your decision. The latter

For hundreds of examples of real forms of all kinds, from award letters to professional judgment applications, check out the following site: **www.nasfaa. org/subhomes/ formsbank/ index.html.**

Eliminate the terms *negotiating*, *bargaining*, and *haggling* from your vocabulary: most financial aid administrators cringe at these buzzwords. Replace them with similar but less noxious phrases such as *reevaluation, special circumstances*, and *additional information*.

college, while claiming it does not negotiate financial aid, may be more willing to simply adjust its ratio.

If the school won't budge, at the very least determine what will happen should you lose that outside scholarship. After all, many outside scholarships cannot be renewed. Will the college replace the loss of the scholarship with the original grant aid it offered? Negotiate this detail and get it in writing so your long-term finances are secure.

... While You Can

Although some colleges do openly state that they will consider matching outside offers, you don't have a whole lot of time to haggle. If you are going to make a play for increasing a school's financial aid offer, try to complete all your haggling before the financial aid priority deadlines. At some point, you'll need to sign and submit your award letter to guarantee you receive, at minimum, the college's original offer. After that point, your bargaining chips are few indeed.

9. Shop Around

Once all the bargaining has come to an end, you'll have to make a decision. All those years of hard work and study have now come to this. Which college will you choose? Your decision will hinge on far more than which school offers you the most money.

The Best Deal

Figuring out the best deal might seem like a relatively straightforward task: look at overall college costs and see which school's financial aid award will leave you with the lowest amount of debt upon graduation. The best financial aid awards have a high percentage of gift aid and offer institutional scholarships/grants that you can easily renew. Though rare, some colleges do entice students to enroll by offering one-year-only scholarships that leave students with higher-than-anticipated costs over the course of four years. Make sure you ask which scholarships you've received are renewable and what the criteria are for keeping them.

The Best Decision

Ultimately, you need to choose a college that meets your overall goals. It makes little sense to accept a great financial aid award if the college doesn't offer the classes you want to take. Similarly, you might think the prestige of attending a certain college is an investment worth the added costs of a lesser financial aid package. You should also consider nonfinancial factors. Do you require at least nine months of sun and warm weather? A full scholarship to the University of Minnesota-Duluth, while impressive, may not be enough of a reason to turn down that partial award to Florida State.

10. Choose Your School

When you've finally settled on the right school, you'll need to sign and submit your acceptance letter. You may choose to accept the entire amount of financial aid as listed in the award letter, or you may decline specific parts of the overall package. Certainly you'll want to accept the grants and scholarships. But when it comes to declining loans and work-study, you need to know a few basics before you start trimming the fat.

Nip and Tuck

After getting to this point in the guide, you understand that some loans just don't look like the others. Some loans are low-interest, need-based, and extremely limited, such as the Perkins loan, while others charge a higher interest rate, are not based on need, and are almost always available, such as the unsubsidized Stafford loan or PLUS loan. You'll first need to look at your free aid and determine if it's enough to cover your tuition, fees, and basic living expenses. Just because the college says your COA is $20,000 doesn't mean you'll actually spend $20,000 in the next year. You may be able to get by on substantially less.

Once you've determined what your needs are, plan your borrowing wisely. If you'll need to borrow, decline your PLUS loan and unsubsidized Stafford loans before your Perkins or subsidized Stafford loans. You may even want to decline that subsidized Stafford loan if you think you'll be able to get by. If you ever get to the point where you think you'll need that loan, you can always reapply for it, even in the last semester.

SCHOOLS THAT
Reward Outside Scholarships

The following colleges should be commended for applying outside scholarships directly to loans and work-study before reducing your other free aid.

1

University of Richmond

2

Northwestern University

3

Wellesley College

4

Carleton College

5

St. Olaf College

6

Idaho State University

7

Johns Hopkins University

8

University of St. Francis

9

MIT

10

Reed College

You should decline work-study and the Perkins loan only if you're absolutely sure you won't use them. Once you decline either one of these awards, you'll very likely be unable to get them back. They're just too limited. In fact, most colleges will typically give you one month to find a work-study job after the school year begins before canceling the award. Take advantage of this time before automatically declining the award. Above all, know that declining work-study or need-based loans will *not* result in more grants or scholarships.

A Worst-Case Scenario

Would you ever decline a grant or scholarship? Hypothetically, the answer to that question might be *yes*. Say, for example, you've been awarded an institutional scholarship for $2,000 per year. However, after accepting your award, you also win an outside scholarship, also for $2,000, but for only one year. If the college reduces the amount of your institutional scholarship and states that there is no guarantee you will receive it once your outside scholarship expires, you might want to decline that outside scholarship. In any case, make sure you know all the facts before making a decision, and above all, get everything in writing.

Next Steps

After you've finally accepted that terrific financial aid package, you can finally sit back and celebrate—but not for too long. There's a lot more you need to know about paying for college than simply the ins and outs of financial aid. You need to look at the whole picture and how to take care of those expenses not included in your COA.

9

THE LONG HAUL

"We see first-year students all the time who forget they must complete a FAFSA every year. Many of them wind up losing financial aid they received as freshmen just because they miss the boat."

Anita
Financial Aid Administrator

You've got your dorm room, your roommate, and a station wagon full of supplies—you're ready for college. But you're not in the clear just yet. Even as you're nestling into your new college life, you need to stay on top of your financial aid. For as long as you're a college student, financial aid is going to remain on your very long list of competing priorities. Paying for college is a marathon, not a sprint, and there are great rewards in store for you if you can keep up your momentum—and carefully guard the money you have.

The Extra Money

When you arrive on campus, your biggest question may be what happens to the financial aid in excess of your college bill. For example, if you've received $20,000 in grants, scholarships, and loans, and your tuition and fees total only $12,000, you have roughly $8,000 remaining. This "extra" money is called *overage.*

Payday

Policies for disbursing overage vary from campus to campus. However, most schools apply your financial aid on a term-by-term basis. If your college follows the two-semester system, your bill will be paid once in the fall semester and once more in the spring semester. Using the above example, you would have roughly $4,000 of overage in the fall semester and $4,000 in the winter semester.

Typically, financial aid offices distribute overage in the form of a check, which can be mailed to your permanent address or picked up by you on campus. Some financial aid offices may even offer you the option of electronic funds transfer (EFT). This allows the financial aid office to deposit your overage directly into your checking account. Take advantage of this opportunity if at all possible, since it will keep you from waiting in line or, worse, taking a chance that your check might get lost in the mail.

No Money for You

You need to know about two exceptions to overage disbursements. For first-time borrowers of the Stafford loan program, overage can't be disbursed until *after* thirty days from the beginning of the academic period.

This means that, as a freshman, you may not have your financial aid to pay for certain items when you need it.

The second disbursement exception applies to students who are enrolled for only one academic period. If you are taking classes for only one semester, any financial aid overage will be divided in half and sent to you in two disbursements: half at the beginning of the semester and the remaining half in the middle of the semester.

Wallet on Fire!

So what do you do when you get a $4,000 check in the mail, made out to you? Finally—financial bliss! That FAFSA was good for something after all . . .

Not so fast. How you respond to that first overage check may very well predict your financial well-being over the next four years. If you've never had a personal budget, you might not be able to resist the temptation to immediately start spending that overage on entertainment and shopping. Unfortunately, after twenty pizzas, three pairs of shoes, and one ski trip, your excess financial aid might be a hazy, fond memory. And coming up with a way to pay for the next two-months'-worth of rent, food, and utilities might get in the way of why you went to college in the first place: studying to earn that all-important degree.

Financial Counseling

These days, colleges understand that students need all the help they can get when it comes to using money wisely. This means that on many campuses you can find studying assistance and career advice as well as personal financial counseling. Iowa State University, for example, has a financial counseling clinic that offers free instruction on topics like personal budgets, managing credit cards, debt management, and even investing. Before you spend a dime of that overage, make sure you find out if your college offers similar services.

Make sure the financial aid office has your correct permanent address, which in many cases is your parents' address. If you don't live with your parents and have moved into an apartment or house, be sure to change your permanent address as quickly as possible.

Cut Big Costs

Although colleges might be more than happy to teach you how to balance your personal budget, they may be less inclined to reveal the secret ways of cutting any costs that may affect their bottom line. After all, colleges have their own budgets to balance, and inexperienced students help provide much of their revenue. With tuition already reaching outrageous heights, you definitely don't want to spend any of your hard-earned cash if you don't have to.

Buy Three, Get One Free

What if someone offered you a way to cut your overall college costs by over $20,000? You'd listen, right? The logic is fairly simple: no law states that you have to take four years to earn a bachelor's degree. In fact, many schools offer specific plans that allow you to earn your four-year degree in three years.

Hood College in Maryland, for example, offers "Accelerated Program Options," which allow students the opportunity to earn a bachelor's degree in three years, or two bachelor's degrees in four years. If you have a 3.0 GPA and scored 530 on both the verbal and math sections of the SAT, Northern Arizona University will offer you admission into one of its three-year degree programs. Regis College in Massachusetts offers twelve three-year degree programs, including Biology, Psychology, and Theater. Talk to your college and find out if it offers a similar plan.

Do It Yourself

Don't worry if your school doesn't explicitly offer a three-year bachelor's degree option. By taking an extra class each semester, transferring credits through testing, and attending college over the summer, you may find you can earn all the credits you need for graduation anyway. You'll need to have a clear understanding of the graduation requirements of your major.

Even more important, however, you'll need to have a clear understanding of the risks related to accelerating your degree. Many students have loaded up on classes in their first semester with every intention of graduating early only to falter under the heavy demands of college life. As you'll see in a moment, you might pay a heavy financial aid cost for dropping classes after the start of the semester.

Be On Time

Even if you have no interest in a three-year option, you should at least try to graduate on time. Many colleges offer "four-year guarantees," which pledge that students can earn a bachelor's degree in a timely fashion . . . or the colleges will pick up the extra costs. Every guarantee comes with a bit of fine print, but you should still check out these plans.

At Emporia State University in Kansas, for example, students who participate in the four-year guarantee program receive additional advising support and assured spots in the classes they need to graduate. If the student completes the terms of the contract but is still unable to graduate in four years, Emporia State will pay any additional tuition needed to complete the degree. Many other colleges have similar plans.

These deals mean a lot at public colleges, since only 34 percent of those students earn a degree in four or fewer years. At private colleges, 65 percent graduate in four or fewer years.

A BA in Two?

The University of San Francisco offers advice on how to earn your bachelor's degree in two years. This requires a heavy portion of transfer credits, as well as CLEP tests, co-op education credits, and University of San Francisco "Portfolio Essays," which offer up to thirty credits tuition-free for writing about how your life experiences apply toward your education.
Visit **www.cps. usfca.edu/ prospective /2_year.html** for more information.

10

EXAMPLES OF
Potential Free Loot

Colleges sometimes serve up a smorgasbord of free stuff and services.

1 Public transportation: Full-time students at the University of California-San Diego can ride for free on local city buses.

2 Celebrity sightings: Universities are known for bringing in top-tier speakers for anything from English classes to graduation.

3 Tax preparation: Winona State University students can receive free tax advice through the Volunteer Income Tax Assistance program.

4 Legal advice: Full-time Southern Illinois University students can access free legal assistance through a special agreement with the local legal community.

5 Lessons: Want to learn ballet, yoga, or knitting? Students at Lewis and Clark College have a "Free University" that offers a wide range of traditional (and not-so-traditional) subjects at no cost.

6 Laptops: Seton Hall University makes sure all students can take their lessons on the go by providing laptop computers.

7 Culture: If you have a University of Massachusetts student ID, you get free admission to the Boston Museum of Fine Arts.

8 Books: The University of Pennsylvania has a link to more than 20,000 free books (**onlinebooks.library.upenn.edu**).

9 Bikes: Michigan State University has a "free bike" program recently started by students and faculty.

10 Stuff: The University of Rochester hosts an online message board where free stuff regularly finds its way to needy students.

Cut Small Costs

Remember that your COA is just an estimate of your tuition, fees, books, room, board, and miscellaneous expenses. If you manage to beat that estimate, you might wind up with a surplus of money at the end of the year. The following advice should help get you on the right track.

Credit—Beware

Many college campuses bear a remarkable resemblance to open-air markets, with things for sale around every corner. Of all the friendly people you'll meet in the next four years, the friendliest are also, perhaps, the most dangerous: credit card reps. Sure, they'll give you a free T-shirt and maybe even a water bottle, but if you fall into their trap, you'll wind up giving them a lot more than they give you. In fact, *the average college student graduates with more than $2,000 in credit card debt.*

Credit cards have their benefits, but some students are far better off avoiding them altogether. Don't like to carry cash? Most banks offer debit cards that provide credit card convenience with a pay-as-you-go mentality. Desperate for a little extra to get you through an emergency? Talk to your financial aid office about an emergency loan or the possibility of increasing your student loans. Dying to double your wardrobe? You'll be happy to know most college students dress down. Way down.

Gear Envy

Technology for college can cost you, but there are many ways to save. If you're moving into the college dorm, check how much local and long distance phone charges will set you back. It might be cheaper for you to join your parents' cell phone plan. In fact, this is now so common

Resist the Urge to Splurge

When you see how much textbooks actually cost, you won't have to dress up in brand-new clothes to feel like a millionaire. Who else but the rich and famous would spend $150 for a history book on the rise of the Italian city-states during the Renaissance?

You can save potentially hundreds of dollars by purchasing used textbooks online. Visit **www.barnesandnoble.com** and click the "New & Used Textbooks" link.

that some college dorms have stopped offering long-distance phone coverage altogether.

You should also call your college before you rush out and buy a computer. Not only do some colleges require specific technology, such as laptop computers, but some also provide this technology at substantial discounts. A few even provide the technology for you.

Keep Up

Each year, thousands of students find out the hard way that what the financial aid office giveth, it can taketh away. A financial aid award is a contract, and when students accept federal financial aid they must meet certain academic standards. The Department of Education has established a strict set of guidelines, known as "Return of Title IV Funds," that requires financial aid offices to return federal financial aid when students don't live up to their part of the bargain.

For example, if a student receives financial aid to take twelve credits and then drops out of college for the semester after cashing the overage check, that student is spending money to which he or she is no longer entitled. Similarly, if a student receives financial aid for twelve credits but then fails each of his or her classes, that financial aid has gone to waste. Paying college costs for the long haul means understanding how to avoid financial aid blunders like these.

You Take It, You Buy It

Colleges are like department stores with unfavorable return policies. In other words, they don't like to give you your money back should you wish to return their product. In fact, after you've attended classes for 60 percent of the academic period, they won't return any money at all to you if you decide to withdraw. Even if you withdraw before that 60 percent point, you won't receive a full refund. At most schools, the amount of your refund drops approximately 10 percent per week. At Dartmouth, for example, if you withdraw during the fourth week of the term, you'll receive only a 50 percent refund. If you withdraw a week after that, you'll receive only a 25 percent refund. After that, you'll receive nothing at all.

There are other consequences to withdrawing from classes: the timing could have a dramatic impact on both your current and future financial aid situation. Federal regulations require that if you drop out before completing 60 percent of the semester (or quarter), you may have to repay part of your financial aid. Financial aid administrators use a formula to determine exactly how much money you'll need to return, based on how many total days make up the college's semester or quarter, how many days you actually attended before withdrawing, and how much, if any, refund you are entitled to from the college. The financial aid office will walk you through this complicated formula. Always speak to them if you're considering dropping a class.

Academic Progress

Sticking out a class means more than just showing up. Colleges have very strict academic progress policies that students must meet in order to remain eligible for financial aid. Though these policies vary slightly from school to school, the most common requirements are that students must maintain a 2.0 cumulative GPA and must complete at least two-thirds of all the classes in which they enroll.

If you violate this Satisfactory Academic Progress (SAP) policy, you have to appeal to the college to have your financial aid reinstated. Generally, financial aid offices will send you a letter should you fall into a SAP violation, but don't wait. If you think your grades may drop you below a 2.0, contact the financial aid office. Part of successfully appealing for your financial aid is making a good-faith effort to address your problems. The financial aid staff will remember and appreciate your honesty.

"When I received a letter from the financial aid office telling me I might lose my grants, I was devastated. But the financial aid counselor walked me through my Satisfactory Academic Progress appeal and I developed a plan to get my grades back on track—without losing my financial aid."

Cara, 19

NSLDS

Many students mistakenly believe that they can leave their problems behind simply by starting over at a new college. However, all college financial aid offices communicate with each other via the National Student Loan Data System (NSLDS). No matter where you go, you'll have to either repay past financial aid to which you were not entitled and/or meet the requirements for satisfactory academic progress before you can receive any federal financial aid at your new school.

The Right Decisions

The Department of Education has a strict policy regarding substance abuse, and drug offenses can completely eliminate a student's chances of receiving financial aid. The law states that anyone convicted of an offense involving the possession of a controlled substance will lose all federal financial aid eligibility for a period of one year from the date of the conviction. A second offense will result in the loss of financial aid eligibility for two additional years. After a third offense, the student loses financial aid eligibility indefinitely.

The penalties for selling controlled substances are even harsher. The first offense will result in a two-year ineligibility period. A second offense results in the indefinite loss of financial aid. If you should ever face the prospect of a controlled substance violation, you should talk with the financial aid office immediately. Though the penalties are severe, the Department of Education does allow for financial aid reinstatement in some cases where a student successfully completes a drug rehabilitation program.

Keep Looking

Your search for financial aid shouldn't end after you receive that first award letter. Financial aid is still out there! Believe it or not, some foundations even reserve financial aid exclusively for upperclassmen.

Your Major

Once you choose a major, you'll discover the wonderful world of the departmental scholarship. College departments reserve these funds exclusively for capable students who have decided to major in their respective fields. For example, if you declare yourself an engineering major at the University of Auburn, you now have access to more than 100 scholarships that aren't available to the general student body.

You shouldn't choose a major prematurely, but if you have a good idea of what you'd like to study, make sure you check in with the appropriate department on campus. They should be able to provide you with a list of any scholarships reserved exclusively for their students.

Excess Aid

If you missed any financial aid deadlines at the beginning of the year, you should stay on the lookout for any extra campus-based aid. As you may recall, colleges disburse some financial aid, such as work-study and the SEOG, on a first-come, first-served basis. Fortunately for you, some students decide later on that they don't want that assistance (such as students who decide not to work), and some must return it because they withdraw from class. In many cases, this money becomes available once again to the general student population.

To benefit from this new pot of financial aid, you need to set up a clear line of communication. Ask the financial aid office how and when returned campus-based assistance gets redistributed to students. Some colleges start a list of interested students, and you'll want your name to be right at the top.

Weave Your Web

One of the scholarship search engines listed in Chapter 4, "The Free Money," will actually send you periodic email messages alerting you to new scholarships, including those for upperclassmen. FastWeb provides not only a scholarship database tailored to your individual needs but also keeps track of upcoming deadlines and then sends these to your inbox.

To sign up for this service, visit **www.fastweb.com**.

Friends in Higher Ed Places

You'll probably learn this secret from your academic advisors: make a good impression on your teachers, and your GPA will soar. The same can be said of financial aid. Many college professors have access to departmental

If your campus has no Alternative Spring Break, you might be interested in starting your own. For eighteen years, Vanderbilt University's Alternative Spring Break program has excelled in community service and springtime travel. In 2004, Alternative Spring Break students at Vanderbilt traveled to twenty-seven locations in the United States, Canada, and Mexico providing needed services for homelessness, HIV/AIDS awareness, and child welfare. To find out more, visit: **www.vanderbilt. edu/asb/**.

research funds, which they can use in a variety of ways. Make a good impression on your professor and you might wind up with an offer to serve as a research or teaching assistant. At the very least, developing professional relationships with college faculty can lead to strong letters of recommendation, which are crucial for fellowship and grad school applications.

Expand Your Horizons

Don't let a little thing like a limited financial aid award keep you from leaving campus. In spite of the rising cost of a gallon of gas, you have plenty of options if you want to expand your horizons during your college years. With a little creativity, student travel doesn't have to be a drag on your wallet.

Alternative Spring Break

Spring break may be the perfect example of how far college students will go for a little R & R. Tales of mind-splitting headaches, painful dry heaves, and humiliating photos certainly make a traditional spring break sound tempting, and you'll no doubt be tempted to join the masses in the annual migration southward. Spring break can also be very expensive, and, unfortunately, the financial aid office won't pick up the bill.

Fortunately, there are some alternatives to Daytona Beach that still allow you to leave your campus confines for parts unknown. Alternative Spring Break, founded in 1987 by students at Vanderbilt University, combines student travel with volunteer projects. Usually led by students, Alternative Spring Break provides an opportunity to see new places, including foreign countries.

Unlike regular spring break excursions, Alternative Spring Break projects often cover costs, including travel, lodging, and meals. Through fundraising and partnerships with local volunteer agencies, many other Alternative Spring Break projects manage to cover costs on their own. Additionally, some projects count for college credit, adding even greater benefit.

Study Abroad

After your first Alternative Spring Break, you may want to expand your horizons even further. Fortunately, you can use your financial aid to pursue study abroad opportunities in just about any country in the world. True, studying in London or Paris might cost much more than studying at home, but the benefits of this kind of experience far outweigh the costs. Plus, study abroad excursions to some of the more exotic countries of the world can actually wind up costing less than a year at home.

If your college has a study abroad coordinator, he or she should be able to tell you all the financial aid implications. If your college has no study abroad programs, there are other agencies that can arrange this for you. One of the best is called the International Student Exchange Program (ISEP). ISEP facilitates student exchanges all over the world, and its reciprocal exchanges help ensure that your costs will be similar to studying at home. They even offer scholarships. For more information, visit www.isep.org.

Eliminate the Middle Man

Did you know that some foreign universities actually accept federal financial aid directly? The FAFSA website offers a search function that allows you to find all schools, both domestic and foreign, where your Title IV aid (Pell Grants, Stafford loans, etc.) may be used. Visit **www.fafsa.ed.gov/fotw0405/fslookup.htm**, select "2004–2005," then select "Search." In the box for "State," select "Foreign country," and you'll get a list of every eligible foreign school.

Get Your Game On . . . Again

Remember: you have to complete the FAFSA every year if you want to keep receiving financial aid. Since the FAFSA becomes available January 1, you won't have much time after your second semester starts before you need to start thinking about all this stuff again. The good news? The whole process should be easier this time around—you're practically an old pro by now. But don't get too complacent. Nothing hurts more than losing the financial aid you received as a freshman.

Renew the FAFSA

The application process is easier the second time around—and even easier if you completed the FAFSA electronically in your first year. Students who complete the electronic FAFSA have to send in only one signature, whereas students who complete the paper FAFSA have to mail in a new signature every year. If you completed the electronic FAFSA, all you need to do now is point your browser to **fafsa.ed.gov** and click the link titled "Fill out a Renewal FAFSA." As long as you have your PIN, everything should go much quicker. If you've lost your PIN, don't worry. You can request it again by following the instructions on the website.

If you completed a paper FAFSA, you also have the option of completing a renewal FAFSA. The Department of Education typically mails these renewal applications to your permanent address after January 1 each year. Although the paper version of the renewal FAFSA is still slower than the electronic version, it still beats starting from the beginning. However, you would be well advised to switch to the electronic version if at all possible. Remember, timing in financial aid is everything.

Rinse. Repeat.

In addition to completing the paperwork, don't forget the tips for getting a better financial aid package you've learned up to this point. Before you fill out the renewal application, review the advice in previous chapters about reporting your income, and make sure that you report any changes in your family's financial circumstances to the financial aid office as soon as possible. And don't lose too much sleep. By now you know just about all there is to know about paying for college. Of course, there might be a few secrets left to share . . .

10

THE SECRETS

"If there's one thing I wish I knew when I started college, it's that everyone should apply for financial aid—even if you think you make too much."

Jack, 21

10

THINGS YOU GOTTA KNOW
Recap

1 **Chapter 1,** "The Process": Completing financial aid forms early is the best thing you can do to receive more financial aid.

2 **Chapter 2,** "The Long Plan": The 529 college savings plan, especially when established by a nonparental relative, currently offers the best flexibility and least risk for paying for college.

3 **Chapter 3,** "The Short Plan": Know how to reduce your "base year income" and assets to increase your eligibility for student financial aid.

4 **Chapter 4,** "The Free Money": Complete the FAFSA even if you've received other aid. There could be more out there.

5 **Chapter 5,** "The Loans": You may not have to pay back your student loans. Explore all the opportunities.

6 **Chapter 6,** "The State System": State grant requirements are often less strict than the Pell Grant requirements.

7 **Chapter 7,** "The Other Aid": Work-study is a much better source of income than outside employment since work-study wages will not hurt your changes of getting aid in EFC calculation.

8 **Chapter 8,** "The Offer": Professional judgment appeals often lead to an increase in financial aid.

9 **Chapter 9,** "The Long Haul": Students can save thousands of dollars by graduating even a little bit early.

10 **Chapter 10,** "The Secrets": Stay tuned!

Even the best financial counselor might not know about every single loophole, backdoor, strategy, or secret when it comes to something as complex as paying for college. The following gems of financial aid wisdom might make you feel pretty smug—but try to hide it next time you're in the financial aid office. Remember, the financial aid counselor is your friend.

Financial aid counselors know a lot. But read on—you may just wind up knowing more than they do.

Free Advice

Student-lending agencies, the companies that manage Stafford, PLUS, and private loans, have launched a growing network of free college-planning services and resources. This makes sense: these agencies, many of which are nonprofit, need students to borrow in order to stay in business. If you're going to take out a student loan anyway, you might as well take advantage of the benefits.

Call Anytime

NextStudent (**www.nextstudent.com**) offers a range of no-cost financial aid services, including free financial aid advice by telephone. Available in English or Spanish, this free consultation could potentially save you hundreds of dollars if you were considering hiring a private financial aid consultant. Call toll-free: 1-800-299-4639.

You can also visit their website for a free scholarship search engine, tips on improving your financial aid eligibility, and updated financial aid news and headlines. Can't remember to visit the site from week to week? Sign up for NextPath, and NextStudent will email you important news and deadlines.

Pay a Visit

Other lenders offer on-site one-on-one counseling. The Northwest Educational Loan Association (NELA), a nonprofit student loan agency, has taken financial aid planning to a personal level through its Centers for Student Success. Students and their families can visit these centers in Portland and Seattle and receive counseling and advice for free.

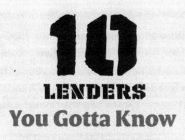

10
LENDERS
You Gotta Know

NextStudent and NELA aren't the only lenders offering free financial advice. These 10 lending agencies offer free services, including advice, publications, and/or scholarship searches, across the country.

1

Northwest Educational Loan Association (www.nela.net)

2

NextStudent (www.nextstudent.com)

3

EdFund (www.edfund.org)

4

SallieMae (www.salliemae.com)

5

College Foundation of North Carolina (www.cfnc.org)

6

EdAmerica (www.edamerica.net)

7

NelNet (www.nelnet.net)

8

New Hampshire Higher Education Assistance Foundation
(www.nhheaf.org)

9

California Higher Education Loan Association
(www.chelastudent loans.org)

10

EduCaid (www.educaid.com)

Can't make the visit to the Emerald City? You can still take advantage of the Center for Student Success web resources, which include a college aid calculator, publications offering advice on finding scholarships, and downloadable webcasts led by financial aid professionals. Most important, it's all free. Visit **www.nela.net**.

Counselors Giving Back

Lending agencies haven't cornered the market on free financial aid advice. Many college financial aid counselors also offer free workshops on applying for financial aid as a pro bono service to the public. Even if you don't plan on attending your hometown university, you might still want to call to see if they'll be offering a public workshop in the future.

A Note of Caution

Of course, each of the above lenders will hope you'll consider them for future services, including student loan consolidation. However, you are under no obligation to do so. As with anything you find on the web, it's generally a bad idea to give out your credit card number, social security number, or any other private information in exchange for "free" services.

If you come across any "free" financial aid seminars coming to your community and arrive to find that they need your credit card for identification purposes only, *it's a scam*. Also, some of these companies may ask that you put down a deposit in order to receive their services. *It, too, is almost assuredly a scam.* Many such financial aid service scams have preyed upon needy families over the years with promises of scholarships and grants. The Federal Trade Commission cracked down on one such business in 2003, ordering NSFA (National Student Financial Aid) to pay $115,000 in fines. But these businesses tend to pop up

A View from the Inside

If you really want to get a view from a financial aid administrator's point of view, check out "Money @ MIT," the financial aid blog written by Daniel Barkowitz, Director of Financial Aid at the Massachusetts Institute of Technology. You can ask questions, leave comments, or just read his thoughts. **http://blogs.mit. edu/barkowitz**

again every year, usually around the time students start thinking about ways to pay for college.

Summer Secrets

In Chapter 7, "The Other Aid," you saw how many colleges have set up programs through which high school students can earn college credit. Since many states will pay summer school tuition for these students, knowing about this secret can save families a small fortune. But college students can also take advantage of summer school options, some of which have long been industry secrets.

Summer Secret #1: Work-Study

From Chapter 7, you know that work-study income will not increase your EFC, which is a good thing! Of course, that might leave you wishing for a work-study position during the summer. Ask and you shall receive. Financial aid offices do, in fact, offer work-study during the summer months, and since fewer students attend college in June, July, and August, you have a greater chance of receiving this campus-based award.

Here's the best part: some colleges, including the University of Washington, Michigan State, and the University of West Virginia, offer full-time work-study awards during the summer. That means even if you don't plan on attending class, you can still receive financial aid in the form of a forty-hour-per-week work-study award. And don't worry if you didn't receive work-study during the regular academic year—you could still have a chance to receive it for the summer. Of course, it bears repeating that none of this income will reduce your eligibility for financial aid in the next academic year. Find out if your college offers work-study during the summer and what you need to do to make it work for you.

Summer Secret #2: Tuition Savings

If you don't want to work during the summer, you can still use summer school to your advantage. Not only is more financial aid available per student during the summer, but using your school's transfer policies may allow you to save on tuition.

Say, for example, you're attending the college of your dreams—but paying the tuition of your nightmares. Perhaps you're attending a public school out-of-state or a pricey private college. In either case, you should look into the possibility of taking cheaper courses at your hometown community or technical college, then transferring those credits to use toward your degree. By taking just a moderate number of courses each summer, you could potentially save thousands of dollars.

Summer Secret #3: Loan Bonus

Some students might attend summer school if only they thought they could receive additional Stafford loans to do so. But remember: your Stafford loan eligibility increases after you attain sophomore and junior status. Based on how many hours you've completed during the year, you might be surprised to find you're suddenly eligible for an additional $875 in Stafford loans following your first year of college and an additional $2,000 of Stafford loans following your second year. Double check the credit requirements with your financial aid office and don't give up on student loans as a means of paying for college during the summer.

SAP Secrets

In Chapter 9, "The Long Haul," you read about the importance of maintaining good grades. The Department of Education requires that each college establish a Satisfactory Academic Progress (SAP) policy for all federal financial aid recipients. If you should somehow fail to meet these SAP policies, you'll need all the help you can get in order to keep your grants, loans, and work-study.

SAP Appeals

If you are told to submit an appeal due to Satisfactory Academic Progress violations (they might even refer to you as a SAP—financial aid counselors get their laughs any way they can), it is survivable, but you have to take it seriously. A clear, concise letter, typed and checked for spelling errors, is absolutely critical. When it comes to supporting documents, more is definitely more. In the event that you are called before the committee for a face-to-face appeal, treat it like a job interview.

Financial aid officers will exercise professional judgment in determining whether or not you'll keep your financial aid and what rules you'll have to follow until you are no longer in violation of SAP policies. Above all, remember that financial aid administrators are just like people (well, practically indistinguishable, anyway). They are subject to the same fits of anger and happiness as anyone else. When you approach the front desk with a pleasant attitude and are clearly intent on getting your grades and attendance back in order, then it is much more likely that the financial aid administrator will bend over backwards to help you.

Sample Letter of Appeal

December 12, 2004

Satisfactory Academic Progress Committee
Office of Student Financial Aid
101 College Dr.
College Place, NV 89101

As outlined in the Satisfactory Academic Progress guidelines, please forward this letter to the Appeals Committee. I will attempt to describe in detail the reasons I have not met my academic goals this semester and what steps I will take to ensure I regain my prior good standing. I understand that the responsibility for keeping my financial aid lies with me.

I made the decision in November to take a second part-time job in order to have some more available money to cover expenses. I have attached a letter from my parents that explains the financial difficulties they have gone through now that I am attending college. Still, I took on additional employment at a time when I felt my grades were stable, but soon found that I could not handle both my workload and my studies. Unfortunately, by the time I realized this, my grades had already fallen to a point that I was forced to withdraw with nonpassing grades.

I have taken two steps to keep this from happening again. First of all, I have visited my academic advisor for assistance. She and I have developed a time management plan that will help me balance both work and school. I have attached a letter of support from her, along with my plan.

In addition, I have asked, and was granted permission by my on-campus employer, to increase my hours by five each week. This will allow me to quit my off-campus job and have more time to devote to my studies, while still meeting my financial obligations. My employer has attached a letter supporting my new work schedule.

I remain focused on earning my degree. If given a chance to have my financial aid reinstated, my grades will become my first priority. In addition, I am also open to any additional resources that the Appeals Committee might recommend for students who are attempting to balance work and school.

Thank you for your consideration of my appeal.

Kevin Jahnsen

Kevin Jahnsen

10
DEADLY SINS
Of the SAP Appeal

1. **Undressed for the occasion:** If you come before the committee without shoes or a shirt, you might as well head on back to the beach. The SAP appeal is just like a job interview. Dress like thousands of dollars are at stake.

2. **Anger mismanagement:** Sure you're angry. Financial aid counselors can feel your pain. They can also add to it. Be nice.

3. **Information underload:** "Look, dude, I'm not sure why you've taken my money from me or why I'm here, so could you just, like, give me back my Pell Grant?" Next.

4. **Unexcused absence:** Financial aid counselors will make a decision in your absence. Be on time for your appointment.

5. **The nutty professor:** If you submit an eloquent letter about how your teacher gave you an F because he just didn't understand the real you, the financial aid counselors will just shake their heads. Don't play the blame game.

6. **Leaving it all behind:** Think threatening to leave the college will help get you what you want? Not likely. In the world of federal financial aid, all academic progress problems are flagged in a big national database called the NSLDS. The folks at the next school won't give you any aid, either.

7. **Taking your medicine too soon:** Okay, so you put it all together, and the financial aid committee rejected your appeal. But it's not really over till the director of financial aid says it's over, so if you have a good case, take it all the way to the top.

8. **Man without a plan:** Every good appeal explains not only why you've fallen behind but also how you're going to get back on track. Make sure you show the appeals committee you've got a plan.

9. **Guilty of nonsupport:** You might think that with a face like yours, the committee is sure to believe anything you say. Better play it safe and provide a few letters of support, just in case.

10. **Not stopping for directions:** Financial aid counselors love their policies and procedures and can be very picky about students who don't follow directions for filing appeals. Dot your *i*s and cross your *t*s if you want Uncle Sam to keep footing your bill.

Put It All Together

Many of the financial aid strategies in Chapters 1–9 can be combined in ways that will further increase their value. You know, for example, that wages from AmeriCorps programs, like work-study, do not impact your EFC. You know that in-state tuition can save you thousands of dollars over out-of-state tuition. You know that colleges often give class credit for life or work experience. Take a look at the following case study to see how one student maximized all his financial aid options.

Case Study: Financial Aid Triple Play

A student from Montana wants to study at a public college in Washington State. As a nonresident, however, his tuition would be approximately $7,000 per year higher than in-state tuition, meaning he would pay nearly $30,000 more for college over four years. This student finds out about residency requirements and finds that he must live and work within the state for at least one year.

Enter AmeriCorps. This national service program, with positions in all fifty states, offers full-time employment and a $4,725 education award that can be used to either pay directly for college costs or repay student loans. The student from Montana takes a position tutoring kids in a Washington State elementary school, which is appropriate since he wants to become a teacher.

At the end of the year, the student meets the requirements for residency but decides to perform one more year of service, earning an additional $4,725 for college in the form of a second AmeriCorps education award. Before even attending college, he now has more than $9,000 in financial aid and will pay nearly $30,000 less for college by earning state residency.

Even better, none of the student's income will negatively impact his financial aid, since AmeriCorps wages are exempt from EFC calculation. Plus, the AmeriCorps education award comes with an unusual benefit: recipients have up to seven years to redeem the money.

A Smart Move

This triple play is significant mainly because of the gift aid to self-help ratio, which you learned about in Chapter 4, "The Free Money," and

Chapter 8, "The Offer." Most colleges would consider the AmeriCorps education award as gift aid, meaning that it could potentially reduce the amount of institutional scholarships or grants you would receive. But since you can use the AmeriCorps education award to repay student loans, a better strategy would be to take out a Stafford or Perkins loan, which would count toward the self-help portion of the student aid ratio. And since you would be repaying the loan upon graduation with your AmeriCorps education award, it would essentially serve to increase the amount of gift aid you could receive in college.

Save Even More

This same student could very likely apply for and receive college credit for his life experience. AmeriCorps members at the Evergreen State College, for example, have received as many as forty-five credits for their experience, which is the equivalent of a full year of college. The student in this example has just reduced the amount of time needed to earn a degree, saving even more money. Plus, even though these credits are worth a great deal, it's the kind of financial aid that doesn't impact your other financial aid, either now or in the future.

None of this even takes into consideration the student's potential for earning scholarships based on community service, or the fact that more than thirty colleges offer matching scholarships to recipients of the AmeriCorps education award. Nor does it take into consideration that the student is starting college two years older. Because of the FAFSA's age requirements for independency status, these additional two years might allow the student the opportunity to qualify for need-based financial aid for at least one or two years, since parental income is no longer considered once a student reaches age twenty-four.

Secret (of) Service

AmeriCorps, when combined with the education award, matching scholarships, and college credit, makes for a great financial aid strategy. But many college students have found that service can be very rewarding in other ways. Even if you don't participate in AmeriCorps, many other organizations exist to reward you for all your good deeds.

Money for a Worthy Goal

If you live in California and dream of launching a career in social justice or peace, the New Voices Fellowship (**newvoices.aed.org**) will help you realize those aspirations. What's the financial aid secret? In addition to receiving a salary of around $35,000, you'll also qualify for student loan repayment assistance of up to $6,000 per year, a professional development account of up to $1,500 per year, and $1,000 to expand your professional networking opportunities.

If you don't live in California, don't despair—the Echoing Green Fellowship (**www.echoinggreen.org**) is equally committed to helping you realize your vision for social change. Successfully pitch your ideas to this annual competition and you'll have taken a major first step toward making the world a much better place. You can apply by yourself for a two-year fellowship worth $60,000 or team up with another social entrepreneur for a two-year, $90,000 award. Either way, everyone comes out ahead.

Service Awards and Scholarships

Receiving your just desserts for your good deeds does not always demand that you take on a full-time social justice project, however. At twenty-five schools, the Bonner Scholar program (**www.bonner.org**) provides financial aid each year to students engaged in service. Bonner scholars also receive support to pursue their career and academic interests, as well as the opportunity to develop leadership skills.

Youth Action Net (**www.youthactionnet.org**) will also recognize your achievements in promoting social change with a $500 award. Similarly, the Do Something Foundation (**www.dosomething.org**) awards up to $10,000 each year to young people who have made a difference. And Youth Service America (www.ysa.org) recognizes young leaders through its Harris Wofford Award, as well as $1,000 in start-up funds through its Youth Venture Funding Program.

It's no secret: no matter what your destination, if you look hard enough you'll likely find out that someone with a little bit of money wants to help you get there.

Field of Dreams

Yes, being a lawyer is a worthy profession, not to mention one of the best ways to appear on CourtTV. But other professions that have received far fewer favorable television shows are just as worthy. Take teaching, for example. True, you probably won't walk away with a shoe endorsement, but at least one national organization strives to support the development of future teachers. Teach for America (www.teachforamerica.org) offers a great incentive to students from all majors who might never have considered teaching as a profession.

Teach for America will place its participants in needy school districts at regular teacher salaries, provide up to $4,725 to repay student loans, and help students receive deferment of their student loans while in the program. In addition, Teach for America has established partnerships with many graduate schools to allow participants to earn a master's degree in education.

You've Got a Friend

Colleges have recently begun to stress the importance of mentoring for incoming students. Mentors, usually upperclassmen or instructors, help new students navigate their first year by providing advice, sharing their own college experiences, and sometimes just offering an open ear. In Washington State, for example, the Gates Foundation has partnered with the Washington Education Foundation (www.waedfoundation.org) to

Pennies for Your Thoughts

With all the term, thesis, and capstone papers ahead of you, writing for fun might be the last thing on your mind. However, if you do enjoy writing, you might as well turn a profit. "Poets & Writers" (www.pw.org) offers links to financial resources, including grants, fellowships, and contests.

provide both scholarships and mentoring opportunities at fifty-one colleges. Participating colleges partner scholarship recipients with individuals who can help with the high school-to-college transition.

At John Jay College in New York, first-year students are paired with upperclass honor students in the Freshmen Peer Mentoring Program. These mentors host weekly events, workshops, and sporting activities so that new students can become familiar with the college community. They even organize classes on financial planning and searching for scholarships.

College students who become mentors typically do so for altruistic reasons, but some schools do repay that kindness in the form of college credit—and, in some cases, cash. Peer mentors at Portland State University in Oregon can receive college credit and also receive an Oregon Laurels scholarship that pays in-state tuition up to twelve credits, plus a monthly stipend of $420. Peer mentors at Weber State University in Utah receive college credit for their first stint and a stipend/scholarship for reenlisting as a mentor. And students at the University of Alaska can receive a biweekly stipend, a dormitory discount, and a $150/semester credit for serving as peer mentors.

Now Go Gently . . .

As the saying goes, "A little knowledge is a dangerous thing." Armed with what you now know about paying for college, you're practically lethal. You should be banned in forty-eight states. In fact, your biggest concern now is being arrested for "impersonation of a financial aid officer." Yes, indeed, the student has in fact become the master. The circle is complete.

Enjoy your time on campus. But be sure and lock up *10 Things You Gotta Know About Paying for College* in a safe place before you head out. You wouldn't want the secret source of all your financial aid power to fall into the wrong hands.

ABOUT THE AUTHOR

Brandon Rogers has worked for nearly ten years as a financial aid counselor and researcher, most recently at Evergreen State College in Olympia, Washington. In 2000, based on his experience as an AmeriCorps member, he was awarded a Western Association of Student Financial Aid Administrators research grant and a Corporation for National Service Fellowship. His research findings led to changes in the Free Application for Federal Student Aid, helping thousands of students nationwide save millions of dollars in lost federal financial aid. He earned his master's degree in education at the University of South Carolina and continues to advocate for students, most recently by speaking at the last four Points of Light National Conferences on Volunteerism and Community Service in Minneapolis, Salt Lake City, Baltimore, and Kansas City. He is currently a college administrator in Tacoma, Washington.

ACKNOWLEDGMENTS

Every financial aid administrator with whom I've worked has contributed in little ways to the development of this guide. By living up to the profession's noble mission of ensuring equal access to a higher education, you prove that students today have no greater friend than the financial aid counselor. To that list of financial aid professionals, I would include this book's editor, Margo Orlando, who, for better or worse, now knows enough obscure acronyms to pass as a genuine FAA. Welcome to the club. (Lifetime membership, I'm afraid.)

This guide is dedicated to the thousands of men and women who enrich themselves and their communities each year through the AmeriCorps program, which has awarded its members over $1 billion in student financial assistance since 1994.